FUN

ENGLISH

BOOK #5
Poetry & Novel
Study

Adriana Fishta-Bejko

To order additional copies of this book, contact:
Xlibris Corporation
1-888-795-4274
www.Xlibris.com
Orders@Xlibris.com
92195

CONTENTS

THEME #1

Language Structure

THEME #2

Special People Special Deeds

Message for the student

This book is designed for intermediate level EAL students, who know the basic structures of English from Fun English, Book 1-4, and who have a vocabulary of roughly 2500-3000 English words. Lessons in Book #5 will add another 500 or more academic words that you will encounter in different mainstream subject textbooks for native speakers of English. The materials consist of highly engaging themes and reading selections of universal interest.

- ❖ **Theme-based approach to reading**. Each of the themes, Language Structure and Special People, consists of authentic classroom dialogues between Mr. Knowitall (the knowledgeable EAL Teacher) and his students from different parts of the world, followed by less than one-page long supplemental reading texts. These units will guide you through various steps of creating a holistic, integrated, and intentional approach to learning. The length of the units and their level of difficulty increases gradually. The texts in the first theme are chosen to be easier to help cover information about the structure of the English language and the content of your discussions is of universal interest. The consecutive lessons become more complex and will help you master new vocabulary, grammatical functions, knowledge about Canada and language skills.
- ❖ **Instructional focus**. In order to help you get acquainted with and master critical reading and writing skills for academic purposes, the materials are organized in a comprehensive pattern that begins with pre-reading questions and discussion, followed by reading exercises, language structure, and ends with writing and technology application exercises.
- ❖ **Pre-reading question.** These questions aim at increasing your interest and motivation to read. A visual clip and the title at the beginning of each unit will help you figure out answers to the pre-reading questions. This helps you recall prior knowledge on the subject being discussed. You will be able to put the logical reasoning

and personal opinion into play to find the answers to those questions all along using words you know and learning more new words.

- ❖ **Recycling vocabulary**. The vocabulary is chosen in a way that helps you learn words that are relevant to your daily communication and learn how to use them in different, new contexts. Each new word introduced in a unit appears in boldface type. On purpose, all the new words are used several times and then recycled systematically throughout the unit and in the units that follow. This approach will help you master and retain the new vocabulary. The book ends with an index of the new words divided into units for your final revision.

- ❖ **Vocabulary enforcement**. The text is followed by a cloze exercise, which helps you read the sentences taken directly from the book and insert the proper words from the list where necessary to complete the sentences. Also, you will find matching and scrambled words exercises very appealing and interesting.

- ❖ **Use new words in a new context**. There is an exercise that gives you a chance to use the new words in a new context but still the words are used in the same meaning as they were first introduced in the lesson.

- ❖ **Reviewing the new words**. In order to give you the chance to use and re-use the new words, new vocabulary words are used in different exercises such as the exercises that use definitions and ask students to find the words or use synonyms and antonyms.

- ❖ **Vocabulary Log**. In each unit, there will be an exercise for you to update and check all the information you have for each new word in the text. You are advised to use information from other readings in mainstream subjects or outside readings to give more details about the words, their plural, verb conjugation, cognates etc. You will be given charts to create "word nests" or to review grammar points. You are required to work with the dictionary and find the word definitions and then use the words in your own sentences.

- ❖ **Reading for comprehension**. Another exercise is Multiple Choice questions. In some of the questions, you are asked to make inferences or discuss the answer with the classmates. This kind of practice is very important and will help you develop reading for comprehension skills.

- ❖ **Main idea**. Three possibilities of ideas are given to you at the end of each lesson and you will choose the one that is the main idea of the story you read. This kind of exercise is important to build good skills for English Language Arts subject.

* **Language Structure point**. Students for whom English is an Additional Language cannot communicate properly unless they learn the main language structure points and functions of the language. To this end, there is a language structure point given as the focus of each unit (degrees of comparison of adjective, articles, possessive case etc.). However, language structure points are not taught in isolation but are embedded in the texts, explained, and then practiced in special exercises.

* **Writing**. Each unit ends with a writing exercise. It may contain writing a personal response, a critique or comparing/contrasting the story with events from your personal experiences. These exercises meet the requirements of the learning outcomes in the official Program of Studies.

* **Use of technology.** You will have a choice to present the writing in an electronic format. There is an exercise that requires you to present your thoughts in the form of Power Point presentation. This is a good opportunity to use your skills in technology to present your thoughts in English. Furthermore, you are encouraged to use the Internet sources to research different sites and documents to support your ideas and presentations.

* **Differentiation: Supplemental reading**. There will be a supplemental reading on the same topic as the text available for you to read and enjoy. Such readings will help you increase your knowledge either about the context of the lesson or about the language structure point discussed in the lesson.

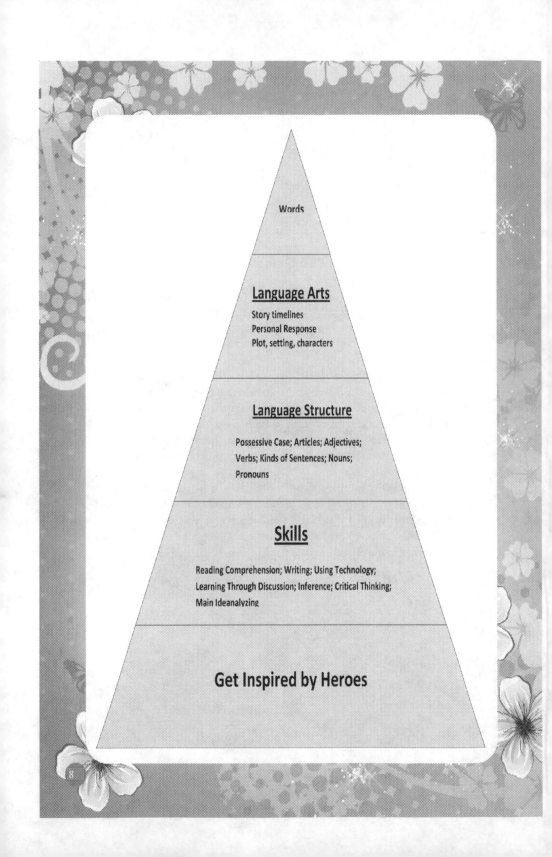

Words

Language Arts
Story timelines
Personal Response
Plot, setting, characters

Language Structure

Possessive Case; Articles; Adjectives;
Verbs; Kinds of Sentences; Nouns;
Pronouns

Skills

Reading Comprehension; Writing; Using Technology;
Learning Through Discussion; Inference; Critical Thinking;
Main Ideanalyzing

Get Inspired by Heroes

REFLECTING ON YOUR LEARNING

(Students will reflect on their learning at the end of each lesson and will confirm their achievement of the objectives. Also they will complete the SKILLS MASTERED COLUMN)

SCOPE AND SEQUENCE

Unit	Supplemental Reading	Skills Mastered	Vocabulary Learned	Expressions	Language Structure
THEME #1 LANGUAGE STRUCTURE					
Lesson 1 An Extraordinary Painter	Kangaroos		Active—38 words Recycled-20 words Passive—27 words	be sure, can hardly wait, are going to . . . , artistic skills	Plural od Nouns
Lesson 2 Our Pets	Unusual Animals		Active—41 words Recycled-32 words Passive—27 words	wake up, a litter of kittens, pick up, take care, bring up	Possessive Case
Lesson 3 Mermaids	Insects		Active—50 words Recycled-24 words Passive—27 words	fall in love, Venn diagram, do not worry, at length, final exams, semester break, works better, come across, have nothing against, according to . . . , looking forward to, until then, next time	Personal Pronouns
Lesson 4 Dragons	Sharks		Active—52 words Recycled-30 words Passive—26 words	to be over, get ready, full of . . . , through ages, each other, long before, digital age, make a point, social media	Degrees of Adjectives
Lesson 5 Active Living or Couch Potato?	Soccer		Active—41 words Recycled-24 words Passive—21 words	couch potato, make dirty, waste basket, instead of, have lunch, take a break	Declarative, Negative & Interrogative Sentences

Lesson 6 At the Restaurant	Butterflies		Active—54 words Recycled-21 words Passive—23 words	have a sweet tooth, have dinner, save some space for, am not sure, grow up	Identifying verb tenses (1)
Lesson 7 When the Sun Went Away	Kittens		Active—44 words Recycled-22 words Passive—20 words	do(ing) fine, nothing to worry about, speak highly of . . ., clear the throat, grow jealous, go away, be scared, beat drums, ring bells, feel sorry	Identifying verb tense (2)
Lesson 8 Thanksgiving	The Businessman		Active—66 words Recycled-30 words Passive—13 words	be around the corner, on the eve of, due to, be confused, ride a horse	THIS & THAT
THEME #2 SPECIAL PEOPLE, SPECIAL DEEDS					
Lesson #1 Town Hero	River Rescue		Active—38words Recycled-21 words Passive—22 words	weather forecast, bring to a stop, run away bus, get hurt, steering wheel, brake pedal, slow down, make matters worse	Definite & Indefinite Articles
Lesson #2 Vote of Confidence	Letter to Hon. Jean Chretien		Active—49 words Recycled-22 words Passive—26 words	House of Commons, fare share, in terms of . . ., according to . . ., reach a plateau, glass ceiling, change the face of	Direct & Indirect Speech
Lesson #3 A Marathon of Hope	Terry Fox		Active—49 words Recycled-32 words Passive—13 words	estrogenic sarcoma, raise funds, pay attention, shocking news, pass away, live on	Passive Voice & Story Timeline

Lesson #4 A Doctor Without Borders	**China's Beloved Hero**		Active—58 words Recycled-33 words Passive—24 words	set up, stretcher bearer, give up on himself, compression therapy, be aware of, bomb shelter	**Personal Response**
Lesson #5 Braille Alphabet	**The Blind Reader**		Active—49 words Recycled-32 words Passive—13 words	partially sighted, index cards, figure out, (go) went wrong, all of a sudden, things were looking up, top secret, iron out, on their own, take up a cause, get around	**Topic Sentence**
			TOTAL 644 new words	**TOTAL** 71 new expressions	

THEME #1
Language Structure

Lesson #1—An Extraordinary Painter

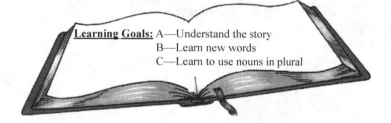

Learning Goals: A—Understand the story
B—Learn new words
C—Learn to use nouns in plural

Language Structure Point: Nouns

<u>Introduction</u> <u>of</u> <u>characters:</u> Our story happens in a school where students learn English as a foreign (EFL) or additional language (EAL). There are many students who learn English in this school and they have many teachers—Mr. Knowitall, Dr. Alba, Miss Lovely, etc. We have already been introduced Mr.Knowitall's students in Book #4 and to Miss Lovely in Book 1-3. Their students have improved their English now and have moved from the Beginner to Intermediate Level. We will get to know Dr. Alba in the Advanced Level books. Now let us go to Mr. Knowitall's class and join the teacher and his students. Here they are:

Mr. Knowitall: (enters the classroom and greets his students) Good morning and **welcome** to our new, **Intermediate Level**. I **am sure** you are interested to know what we will learn in this level and how you will develop more English proficiency skills.

Ben: (very excited) Yes, Mr. Knowitall. I **can hardly wait** to learn new skills and go to the Advanced Level.

Mr. Knowitall: I am glad to see how excited you arc, Bcn. We will learn many new words and stories in the Intermediate Level. They are interesting stories that you will see in the books for your other **subjects**.

Carol: I like our dialogues in class very much. They help me to **practice** the words I learn.

George: (politely) Yes, Carol, I agree with you but before enjoying a dialogue we need to study the vocabulary for that dialogue. Learning the definitions of the words and using them in sentences has been very important for improving my language proficiency.

Monique: What story are we **going to** learn today, Mr. Knowitall?

Mr. Knowitall: Today we are going to talk about a very interesting and **unusual painter.** She is very **famous** for her **artistic skills** (laughs) and she is very unique because there are no other painters like her in the **world**.

Paolo: Does she use a special computer **software** to **paint**, Mr. Knowital?

Mr. Knowitall: No Paolo, she only uses her only her big nose (laughs).

Paolo: (looks **puzzled**) How can she paint with her nose? That is **impossible**.

Mr. Knowitall: That is exactly how she paints. She has developed this skill and people like her paintings very much. Some of your friends will help us expand our knowledge about this unusual painter. I have given them some **information** and they have **created** a story. Let us listen to their story.

Stephen: I was totally **surprised** when I first learned about this unusual painter. The **zoo** in our town has its own painter. She is a fabulous painter. She is an Asian **elephant**. (Everybody looks surprised)

Ming: (continues the story) Her name is Ruby. Ruby paints pictures and people buy them. This is what **happens** every day in this zoo. (Points to Stephen to continue the story)

Stephen: (continues the story) A **zookeeper** lines up **jars** of **paint**. He sets up an **easel** with a large **piece** of **paper** on it. Ruby picks out the colors she wants to use by **pointing** to the jar with her **trunk**. (All students are very attracted to the story)

Ming: (continues the story) Then the zookeeper **dips** a **brush** into the paint. Ruby **curls** her trunk around the brush **handle**. She paints flowers, straight lines, wavy lines, circles, triangles, squares, and circles. This elephant likes to use many colors in her paintings. No two of her pictures are ever alike.

Stephen: (proud of his knowledge continues the story) People like **to own** a picture painted by an elephant because it is so unique. They pay up to $650 for one of Ruby's paintings.

Monique: (very excited) This is an **amazing** story. Thank you for **sharing** it with us you **guys**.

Mr. Knowitall: I am glad you liked it, Monique. How about the others, "Did you like the story?"

(All the students agree that the story was very intersting) OK! Let us work with some questions to see if we understood the story and **analyze** more vocabulary words and **master** them.[1]

Practice Your Knowledge

Exercise #1—Vocabulary study

Task 1—Check the meaning of the following words in your dictionary. Copy the definitions.

Task 2—Find the sentence with the same word from the text and copy it or write your own sentence. Follow the example with the word "skill(s)":

Definition—e. x. **"skill"**—talent and ability to perform something well.

Sentence—I learn many academic words to improve my English skills.

❑ welcome
Definition . . . .
. . . .
Sentence . . . .
. . . .

❑ intermediate
Definition . . . .
. . . .
Sentence . . . .
. . . .

❑ level
Definition . . . .
. . . .
Sentence . . . .
. . . .

---

[1]   Adapted from the story of the elephant in Phoenix, Arizona. To learn more about Ruby check http://en.wikipedia.org/wiki/Ruby_(elephant)

❏ subject

Definition . . . .
. . . .

Sentence . . . .
. . . .

❏ unusual

Definition . . . .
. . . .

Sentence . . . .
. . . .

❏ artistic

Definition . . . .
. . . .

Sentence . . . .
. . . .

❏ famous

Definition . . . .
. . . .

Sentence . . . .
. . . .

❏ world

Definition . . . .
. . . .

Sentence . . . .
. . . .

❏ practice

Definition . . . .
. . . .

Sentence . . . .
. . . .

❏ painter

Definition . . . .
. . . .

Sentence . . . .
. . . .

❑ software
Definition . . . .
. . . .
Sentence . . . .
. . . .

❑ to paint
Definition . . . .
. . . .
Sentence . . . .
. . . .

❑ the paint
Definition . . . .
. . . .
Sentence . . . .
. . . .

❑ puzzled
Definition . . . .
. . . .
Sentence . . . .
. . . .

❑ impossible
Definition . . . .
. . . .
Sentence . . . .
. . . .

❑ information
Definition . . . .
. . . .
Sentence . . . .
. . . .

❑ create(ed)
Definition . . . .
. . . .
Sentence . . . .
. . . .

❏ surprise(d)
Definition . . . .
. . . .
Sentence . . . .
. . . .

❏ zoo
Definition . . . .
. . . .
Sentence . . . .
. . . .

❏ zookeeper
Definition . . . .
. . . .
Sentence . . . .
. . . .

❏ elephant
Definition . . . .
. . . .
Sentence . . . .
. . . .

❏ happen
Definition . . . .
. . . .
Sentence . . . .
. . . .

❏ jar(s)
Definition . . . .
. . . .
Sentence . . . .
. . . .

❏ easel
Definition . . . .
. . . .
Sentence . . . .
. . . .

❏ piece

Definition . . . .

. . . .

Sentence . . . .

. . . .

❏ paper

Definition . . . .

. . . .

Sentence . . . .

. . . .

❏ point to . . . .

Definition . . . .

. . . .

Sentence . . . .

. . . .

❏ trunk

Definition . . . .

. . . .

Sentence . . . .

. . . .

❏ to dip

Definition . . . .

. . . .

Sentence . . . .

. . . .

❏ brush

Definition . . . .

. . . .

Sentence . . . .

. . . .

❏ to curl

Definition . . . .

. . . .

Sentence . . . .

. . . .

❑ the handle
Definition . . . .
. . . .
Sentence . . . .
. . . .

❑ to own
Definition . . . .
. . . .
Sentence . . . .
. . . .

❑ amazing
Definition . . . .
. . . .
Sentence . . . .
. . . .

❑ sharing
Definition . . . .
. . . .
Sentence . . . .
. . . .

❑ guy(s)
Definition . . . .
. . . .
Sentence . . . .
. . . .

❑ to master
Definition . . . .
. . . .
Sentence . . . .
. . . .

❑ to analyze
Definition . . . .
. . . .
Sentence . . . .
. . . .

Exercise #2—Check your understanding of the story. Answer the following questions:

- Who is the famous artist in the story?_____
- What kind of animal is the artist and where does she live?

  _____
- When does the zoo worker dip a brush into the paint and what does Ruby do with the brush? _____
- Where does Ruby live and what do you know about that place?

  _____
- Why do people buy Ruby's paintings? _____
- What makes Ruby a special elephant and a famous painter?

  _____

B

Exercise #3—Find the secret word and write a sentence with it.

mecolew _____

_____

tfosrewa _____

_____

ssbilepoim _____

_____

mosuaf _____

_____

pehelatn _____

_____

Exercise #4—**VOCABULARY BUILDING**-Insert the right word from the list in the blanks in the following sentences. Sentences are taken from the lesson "An Extraordinary Painter". Make the necessary changes to the words.

famous	painter	software	artistic	zookeeper
unusual	subject	to paint	the paint	impossible

create	surprised	master	analyze	handle
amazing	to curl	trunk	easel	to dip
puzzled	world	skills	elephant	

- Then the zookeeper _____ a brush into the paint.
- He sets up an _____ with a large piece of paper on it.
- She is an Asian _____.
- Ruby picks out the colors she wants to use by pointing to the jar with her _____.
- I was totally_____ when I first learned about this unusual painter.
- Today we are going to talk about a very interesting and _____ _____.
- A _____ lines up jars of _____.
- They are interesting stories that you will see in the books for your other _____.
- Ruby _____ her trunk around the brush _____.
- She is very _____ for her _____ _____ (laughs) and she is very unique because there are no other painters like her in the _____.
- Does she use a special computer _____ to _____, Mr. Knowital?
- Let us work with some questions to see if we understood the story and _____ more vocabulary words and _____ them.
- (looks _____) How can she paint with her nose? That is _____.
- This is an _____ story.

Exercise #5:—VOCABULARY BUILDING-Use the words you learned in the lesson "An Extraordinary Painter" in a new context:

to paint	the paint	impossible	create	amazing
famous	software	artistic	zookeeper	unusual
easel	master	world	elephant	analyze
brush				

1. Children can learn to understand a story better when the teacher asks them to _____ a picture.
2. The mother was not happy when the boy put _____ all over his clothes.
3. Have you read the book by this _____author?
4. It is _____ to fail an exam if you study hard.
5. I am taking a course to learn how to use a new_____ program.
6. My brother is a _____ and his job is to take care of the animals.
7. Her _____ _____ skills are famous all over the _____.
8. The painter takes his_____ to the woods _____ a beautiful tree.
9. It is_____ to _____ a story without_____ the new language.
10. The student tells an _____ story about an _____.

Grammar Point—Nouns: are of different kinds and plural forms:

There are two kinds of nouns: **Common Nouns** ex: book, cat, chair, elephant and **Proper Nouns** (names) ex: Ruby, Canada, China, Albania, John.

Nouns can be—a) countable or b) uncountable.

a) **Countable Nouns**—are nouns that can be counted and changed into plural, i.e. most of the nouns in the English language, e. x. house-houses, wife-wives, teacher-teachers

b) **Uncountable Nouns**—are nouns that cannot be counted or changed into plural, i.e. abstract nouns, nouns of materials, e. x. tea, milk, sugar, pity, love, admiration

There are different ways to form the **plural of countable nouns:**
1. Most of the nouns take an "s" ending suffix in plural, ex.: pen-pens, book-books,

2. Some nouns change completely (irregular), ex.: child-children, ox-oxen, mouse-mice
3. Nouns ending in "ch", "s", "x", "sh" take "es" in plural, ex.: coach-coaches, watch-watches, bus-buses, box-boxes, glass-glasses
4. Nouns ending in "y", which is preceded by a consonant, form the plural by adding "ies" to the root of the word, ex.: lady-ladies, country-countries, party-parties BUT "y" does not change if it is preceded by a vowel, e. x.: boy-boys, day-days, toy-toys
5. Some nouns with double "oo" in singular change into "ee" in plural, ex.: tooth-teeth, goose-geese, foot-feet
6. Some nouns ending in "fe" or "eaf" in singular change into "ves" in plural, ex.: wife-wives, knife-knives, leaf-leaves
7. Some nouns can be used only in plural, ex.: trousers, scissors, glasses. To count these nouns we use "one pair of" before the noun, e. x. one pair of trousers—two pairs of trousers; one pair of scissors—two pairs of scissors.
8. Some nouns do not change in plural, ex.: sheep, deer, cattle. When we want to count these nouns we use "one head of" before the noun. One head of sheep—two heads of sheep; one head of cattle-two heads of cattle.
9. The noun "people" is usually considered singular in form but plural in meaning, e. x.: The old people are very wise. Only when "people" means "nation", the noun can be used in plural: people-peoples, e. x.: The peoples of Asia share some common traditions.

Exercise #6—Look at the following sentences and use the correct form of the noun to complete these sentences:

- When I cook, I use two different, sharp_____(knife)
- There is some _____(water) in the tall, glass bottle.
- I left two _____(box) of children books in the car.
- Can you buy two _____(bottle) of milk on your way from school?
- I had two _____(tooth) pulled out the week before school started.
- How many _____(people) speak English in this class?
- These _____(woman) are from Alberta province, Canada.
- There were many _____(country) that took part in the Olympic Games in China.

- Five _____(boy) did not come to school. They were sick.
- Jimmy bought two new _____(trousers) before he left the city.

Homework—Find ten nouns in the lesson and change their number. Follow this example: classroom-classrooms

1. . . . .
2. . . . .
3. . . . .
4. . . . .
5. . . . .
6. . . . .
7. . . . .
8. . . . .
9. . . . .
10. . . . .

Supplemental Reading: Choose the best title for the following short story: a) Small Animals; b) The Kangaroo Rat; c) How Kangaroos Get Water; d) How a Kangaroo Looks

The kangaroo rat is a tiny animal that jumps around like a kangaroo. The rat can leap on his powerful hind legs. His tail is about as long as his body. Kangaroo rats have silky fur of yellow or brown on the under-parts of their bodies and white under-parts. They can stuff food into fur-lined pouches on the outside of their cheeks. They do not need to drink water. They get water from inside themselves when their food combines with the oxygen they breathe. These rats live in the deserts of the southwestern United States of America.

<u>STUDY</u> <u>TIP</u>—**Take responsibility for your study**— Recognize that in order to succeed you need to make decisions about your priorities, your time, and your resources for studying.

<u>SPOT</u> <u>THE</u> <u>MISTAKE</u>—Find the mistakes and fix them. Write the correct sentence:

This zookeeper   is teaching his students . . . .

. . . .

. . . .

. . . .

. . . .

. . . .

. . . .

. . . .

. . . .

<u>REMEMBER</u> <u>THIS</u>—Many words take a prefix. A prefix is a syllable placed before the root of the word to change its meaning. A prefix is a syllable in itself. On the other hand, a suffix is a letter or a word placed at the end of the root of a word to change its meaning.

<u>DID</u> <u>YOU</u> <u>KNOW</u>?—In 1785 B.C., the first calendar composed of 354 days, was introduced by Babylonian scientists.

LANGUAGE BANK—In this lesson you learned:

Active words	Recycled words	Passive words
1. welcome	1. proficiency	1. continue
2. intermediate	2. develop	2. perform
3. level(s)	3. excited	3. academic
4. subject(s)	4. glad	4. prefix(es)
5. unusual	5. dialogue(s)	5. suffix(es)
6. artistic	6. definition(s)	6. syllable(s)
7. famous	7. enjoy	7. root(s)
8. to analyze	8. vocabulary(ies)	8. to place
9. world(s)	9. agree	9. itself
10. practice	10. sentence(s)	10. kangaroo
11. painter(s)	11. important	11. rat(s)
12. software	12. need	12. jump
13. to paint	13. knowledge	13. leap
14. the paint	14. story(ies)	14. powerful
15. puzzled	15. totally	15. hind
16. impossible	16. fabulous	16. tail(s)
17. information	17. proud of	17. search
18. create(ed)	18. because	18. food
19. surprise(d)	19. unique	19. large
20. zoo(s)	20. excited	20. silky
21. zookeeper(s)		21. fur
22. elephant		22. stuff
23. happen		23. pouch(es)
24. jar(s)		24. combine
25. easel		25. oxygen
26. piece		26. breathe
27. paper		27. desert
28. point to		
29. trunk		**Expressions:** am (to be) sure, can hardly
30. to dip		wait, are going to (do) . . . , artistic skills

32

31. brush
32. to curl
33. the handle
34. to own
35. amazing
36. sharing
37. guy(s)
38. to master

Lesson #2—Our Pets

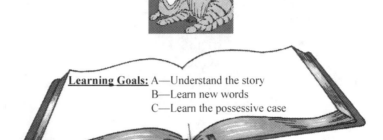

Learning Goals: A—Understand the story
B—Learn new words
C—Learn the possessive case

Language Structure Point: Possessive Case

(It is a beautiful day in the city. Mr. Knowitall is taking his usual **morning walk around** the **neighborhood**. He sees a lot of people walking their dogs. As he is thinking about **today**'s class, he **decides** that it would be interesting to have a discussion **about pets** and different **ways** people **care** about their pets.)

Mr. Knowitall: (enters the classroom with a big **smile** on his **face** and **greets** his students) Good morning my dear friends. I **hope** you are enjoying these **sunny** days as much as I am. How is everybody today?

Ben: I am fine, Mr. Knowitall. This morning I went running with a friend.

Carol: I am **too** **lazy** to **wake up** **early** in the morning and go running. I need to **change** that because it is **better** to have a healthy **lifestyle**.

George: It is difficult for me to wake up early, too. Usually, I exercise in the **afternoon**.

Carol: I have another problem: I feel uncomfortable to run all by myself. People may think I am stupid running around the neighborhood.

Monique: I had the same **problem** before, Carol, but now I am OK. I bought a dog and now I go running with my pet.

Carol: That is a great idea. Where can I buy a pet?

Ming: I can help you with that. I bought my cat in the pet **store**.

Paolo: I have a pet, too. It is a beautiful bird and I like it very much.

Mr. Knowitall: It is interesting that you are talking about pets because my plan was to discuss about the same **topic** today.

Monique: (excited) I like pets very much. Thank you for choosing that topic, Mr. Knowitall.

Mr. Knowitall: I **prepared** a short story about my neighbour Indrit and his cat. I need two volunteers to share the story with us.

Stephen: I would be very happy to read the story for the class, Mr. Knowitall.

Monique: I can read with Stephen, too. I will be Stephen's reading partner.

Mr. Knowitall: That is great. Why don't you each take turns to read the story?

Stephen: That sounds great. I can start with the first sentence. (starts reading from the paper that Mr. Knowitall gives to him). When Indrit's cat, Puffy had a **litter** **of** **kittens**, Indrit put them in his wagon.

Monique: (**picks up** reading) The wagon's **wheels** are small. The boy **picks** the wagon's handle and pulls the wagon along the sidewalk. Kittens' mom, Puffy, is very happy.

Stephen: (reads) Indrit's brother, Nick, helps Indrit **take care** of the kittens. They **cut** kittens' **nails often**. Nick's shoebox has **become** kittens' little bed.

Monique: (continues reading) Indrit keeps the kitten in his own room. They like to play with mother's balls of **yarn**. The boy's room is a warm place for the kitten.

Stephen: (finishes the story) Sometimes, the neighbor's dog **starts barking** when Indrit and his wagon **pass** by but that does not **bother** the kittens. Puffy's babies are healthy and happy. Kittens' health is Indrit's main **concern**. He **promises** to **bring them up safely**.

Carol: That is an interesting story. Now I understand how much fun it is to have a pet. I really like to protect animals from people who may injure them.

Ming: You are right, Carol. It is so much fun to have a pet. If you want, I can show you this afternoon where to buy a pet and the food for your pet.

Mr. Knowitall: Thank you for an **excellent** reading Stephen and Carol. Your pronunciation is very good and it is easy to understand the story that you read.

Practice Your Knowledge

Exercise #1—Vocabulary study

Task 1—Check the meaning of the following words in your dictionary. Copy the definitions.

Task 2—Find the sentence with the same word from the text and copy it or write your own sentence. Follow the example with the word **"morning":**

Definition—the time of the day when the sun comes up until noon

Sentence—I wake up early every morning.

❑ neighborhood

Definition . . . .
. . . .
Sentence . . . .
. . . .

❑ walk

Definition . . . .
. . . .
Sentence . . . .
. . . .

❑ today

Definition . . . .
. . . .
Sentence . . . .
. . . .

❑ decide
Definition . . . .
. . . .
Sentence . . . .
. . . .
❑ about
Definition . . . .
. . . .
Sentence . . . .
. . . .
❑ pet(s)
Definition . . . .
. . . .
Sentence . . . .
. . . .
❑ way(s)
Definition . . . .
. . . .
Sentence . . . .
. . . .
❑ care
Definition . . . .
. . . .
Sentence . . . .
. . . .
❑ around
Definition . . . .
. . . .
Sentence . . . .
. . . .
❑ smile(s)
Definition . . . .
. . . .
Sentence . . . .
. . . .

❑ face(s)
Definition . . . .
. . . .
Sentence . . . .
. . . .

❑ great
Definition . . . .
. . . .
Sentence . . . .
. . . .

❑ hope
Definition . . . .
. . . .
Sentence . . . .
. . . .

❑ sunny
Definition . . . .
. . . .
Sentence . . . .
. . . .

❑ too
Definition . . . .
. . . .
Sentence . . . .
. . . .

❑ lazy
Definition . . . .
. . . .
Sentence . . . .
. . . .

❑ early
Definition . . . .
. . . .
Sentence . . . .
. . . .

❏ change
Definition . . . .
. . . .
Sentence . . . .
. . . .
❏ better
Definition . . . .
. . . .
Sentence . . . .
. . . .
❏ lifestyle(s)
Definition . . . .
. . . .
Sentence . . . .
. . . .
❏ store(s)
Definition . . . .
. . . .
Sentence . . . .
. . . .
❏ problem(s)
Definition . . . .
. . . .
Sentence . . . .
. . . .
❏ plan(s)
Definition . . . .
. . . .
Sentence . . . .
. . . .
❏ topic(s)
Definition . . . .
. . . .
Sentence . . . .
. . . .

❑ choose

Definition . . . .
. . . .

Sentence . . . .
. . . .

❑ prepare

Definition . . . .
. . . .

Sentence . . . .
. . . .

❑ pick

Definition . . . .
. . . .

Sentence . . . .
. . . .

❑ sidewalk(s)

Definition . . . .
. . . .

Sentence . . . .
. . . .

❑ wheel(s)

Definition . . . .
. . . .

Sentence . . . .
. . . .

❑ cut

Definition . . . .
. . . .

Sentence . . . .
. . . .

❑ nail(s)

Definition . . . .
. . . .

Sentence . . . .
. . . .

❑ often
Definition . . . .
. . . .
Sentence . . . .
. . . .
❑ become
Definition . . . .
. . . .
Sentence . . . .
. . . .
❑ start
Definition . . . .
. . . .
Sentence . . . .
. . . .
❑ bark
Definition . . . .
. . . .
Sentence . . . .
. . . .
❑ pass
Definition . . . .
. . . .
Sentence . . . .
. . . .
❑ bother
Definition . . . .
. . . .
Sentence . . . .
. . . .
❑ concern
Definition . . . .
. . . .
Sentence . . . .
. . . .

❑ safely
Definition . . . .
. . . .
Sentence . . . .
. . . .
❑ promise
Definition . . . .
. . . .
Sentence . . . .
. . . .
❑ excellent
Definition . . . .
. . . .
Sentence . . . .
. . . .

Exercise #2—Check if you have understood the story. Answer the following questions:

* Where does Indrit put the kitten? _____
* Which animal is the kitten's mom? _____
* Where do kittens live in Indrit's house? _____
* Who is Nick? _____
* Why are Puffy's kittens healthy and happy? _____

Exercise #3—Find the secret word and write a sentence with it.

❖ teexeclnl_____ . . . .
. . . .
. . . .
. . . .

❖ ohrneigbourhod_____ . . . .
. . . .
. . . .
. . . .

❖ lkdeisaw_____ . . . .
. . . .
. . . .
. . . .

❖ lestyifel_____ . . . .
. . . .
. . . .
. . . .

❖ nrecnoc_____ . . . .
. . . .
. . . .
. . . .

Exercise #4: **VOCABULARY BUILDING**—Insert the right word from the list in the blanks in the following sentences. Make the necessary changes to the words. Sentences are taken from the lesson "Our Pets".

neighborhood	hope	store	topic	prepare
lifestyle	excellent	morning	concern	nails
bark	start	bother	promise	

- Thank you for an _____ reading Stephen and Carol.
- He _____ to bring them up safely.
- Kittens' health is Indrit's main _____.
- Sometimes, the neighbor's dog _____ when Indrit and his wagon pass by but that does not _____ the kittens.
- They cut kittens' _____ often.
- I _____ a short story about my friend Indrit and his cat.
- It is interesting that you are talking about pets because my plan is to discuss about the same _____ today.
- I bought my cat in the pet _____.
- Mr. Knowitall is taking his usual _____ walk around the _____.
- I _____ you are enjoying these sunny days as much as I am.
- I need to change that because it is better to have a healthy _____.

Exercise #5: VOCABULARY BUILDING—Use the words you learned in the lesson "Our Pets" in a new context. Make the necessary changes.

morning	concern	nails	bark	start
bother	promise	neighborhood	hope	store
topic	prepare	lifestyle	excellent	

- He is an _____ singer and a great athlete.
- The mother does not agree with her son's _____and they discuss that problem often.
- John worked all week to _____ for the final exam.
- It was difficult for me to write the essay on that _____ because I had no information.
- They opened a new_____ to sell healthy, organic food.
- We _____ that the weather will be better tomorrow.
- People from the whole _____went out looking for the missing boy.
- Parents are _____ about the future of their children.
- It is important to cut the baby's _____ often because he can scratch his face.
- The dog _____ when strangers come to the house.
- Nick _____learning English when he was in second grade.
- Campers complain about mosquitos because they _____ them.
- John _____ that he will never be late again.

Grammar Point—Possessive Case of Nouns

❖ If two nouns have a relationship of ownership (owner + property) we use Possessive Case, ex. : the desk of the teacher—teacher's desk; the book of the student—student's book; the kittens of Walter—Walter's kittens

Remember—if the noun of the property ends in "s" or is in plural we only add the apostrophe but not the "s" for the possessive case, ex.: box' lid, bus' stop, fox' tail, teachers' meeting, girls' kitten, students' books.

Exercise #6—Use the correct form of the possessive case to complete these sentences:

1. We will meet at 3:00 p.m. in the _____ (office of the teacher).
2. I found this book in _____ (the room of my aunt).
3. He has bought all those _____ (books of children) last year.
4. Where did you find _____ (the bag of your friend)?
5. Can you take me to _____ (the house of Mr. Strauss), please?
6. Where are _____ (the shoes of Mike), Nick?
7. He found _____ (the ring of his mother) in the box.
8. This is the biography of _____ (the mother of Nancy).
9. I took _____ (the job of my father) after he retired.
10. They are living _____ (in the house of my mother) this summer.

Homework—Use the table to write 15 good sentences. Follow the example: Miss **Wong's** favorite food is orange. Miss **Wong's** favorite movie is Titanic. etc.

Name	Favorite ????!!!!	. . . . is
Mr. King	Food	Meat
My mother	Colour	Blue
Mr. Chen	Sport	Soccer

My doctor	Drink	Tea
Miss Tong	Movie	Titanic

Supplemental Reading—Choose the best tittle for the following short story: a) The Inflatable Fish; b) Puffins; c) Puffer Fish d) Unusual Animals

Some fish are able to inflate their bodies like balloons. The common name of such fish is "puffer fish" or "swell fish". Some common puffers live along the Atlantic coast, while others live in tropical waters. Most of the time, the puffer looks like an ordinary fish with a large head, a mouth that appears to have teeth sticking out. When the fish is disturbed, it inflates its stomach with air. After it is inflated, it floats belly upward on the surface of the water until the danger has passed. It may blow itself to twice its normal size. The name "puffer" may be confused with the word "puffin", which is actually an odd-looking bird that lives in the Arctic.

STUDY TIP—**Put first things first**—follow up on the priorities you have set for yourself. Do not let other things distract you from achieving your goals.

SPOT THE MISTAKE—Find the mistakes and fix them. Write the correct sentence:

This fish inflates its body when people disturb it . . . .

. . . .
. . . .
. . . .
. . . .

REMEMBER THIS—When you use a computer, use only one space following periods, commas, commas, semi-colons, colons, exclamation marks, question or quotation marks.

DID YOU KNOW?—The most commonly used letter of the English alphabet is "E".

LANGUAGE BANK—In this lesson you learned:

Active words	Recycled words	Passive words
1. neighborhood	1. city	1. inflate
2. walk	2. beautiful	2. inflatable
3. today	3. usual	3. common
4. decide	4. think	4. along
5. about	5. interesting	5. tropical
6. pet(s)	6. discussion	6. waters
7. way(s)	7. different	7. ordinary
8. care	8. enter	8. appears
9. around	9. enjoy	9. sticking out
10. smile(s)	10. run	10. disturb
11. face(s)	11. need	11. stomach
12. great	12. because	12. air
13. hope	13. healthy	13. belly
14. sunny	14. exercise	14. float
15. too	15. difficult	15. upward
16. lazy	16. afternoon	16. surface
17. early	17. cat	17. danger
18. change	18. bird	18. pass
19. better	19. share	19. blow

20. lifestyle(s)
21. store(s)
22. problem (s)
23. plan(s)
24. topic(s)
25. choose
26. prepare
27. pick
28. sidewalk(s)
29. wheel(s)
30. cut
31. nail(s)
32. often
33. become
34. start
35. bark up
36. pass
37. bother
38. concern
39. safely
40. promise
41. excellent

20. sentence
21. wagon
22. handle
23. own
24. yarn
25. sometimes
26. main
27. characteristic
28. pronunciation
29. easy
30. understand
31. protect
32. injure

20. twice
21. normal
22. confuse
23. actually
24. odd-looking
25. essay
26. organic
27. complain

Expressions: wake up, a litter of kittens, pick up, take care, bring

Lesson #3—Mermaids

Learning Goals: A—Understand the story
B—Learn new words
C—Learn how to use pronouns

Language Structure Point: Pronouns

(Mr. Knowitall and his students have discussed about interesting **creatures** that live in the sea. Students enjoyed the **supplemental** reading about the inflatable fish. So, Mr. Knowitall has decided to **continue** talking about some **legends** **related** to the sea. Also, he wants to **compare** the legends from different countries.)

Mr. Knowitall: Good morning, **Folks.** I have been thinking about that inflatable fish. What an interesting story it was! I really enjoyed reading it. How about you?

Stephen: I enjoyed reading that story, too. We have **the same** kind of fish in my country.

Ming: It was an amazing story but sometimes I do not know where the story ends and the legend begins. We have many legends about sea creatures in my country, too.

Ben: It is the same with us. When we were children, we were told stories about **mermaids** that come from the **ocean** and **fall in love** with **handsome** guys.

Carol: That is very interesting, Ben. We have the same legend about the mermaids in my country. It would be a good **idea** to compare your legend with our legend and see the **similarities** and the **differences** that our stories contain.

George: You are **sounding** like my Language Arts' teacher, Carol. She talks about compare and **contrast** and something **called Venn Diagram** all the time. I have **never** understood what that is.

Mr. Knowitall: Don't worry about compare and contrast and the Venn Diagram now, George. We will discuss that topic **at length** in a lesson in **Theme** #2 of this book. **However**, I am very **intrigued** by Carol's **proposa**l about comparing legends from different countries. **Maybe** we can start a **project** to **collect** legends from different countries and **then** compare **them**. What do you think?

Monique: That would be an excellent idea but I am concerned as we are very **busy** now because we have to prepare for **final exams**. Can we do that **during** our **semester break**?

Paolo: I like the idea of collecting legends but, like Monique, I have final exams this **month** also. Semester break would be great time for me, too.

Carol: The same with me. I would have more **time** during the semester break.

Mr. Knowitall: Sounds like semester break **works better** for everybody. Let us think about that project **later** then.

George: (gives his opinion) **Meanwhile,** can we **hear** something about one of these sea creatures, Mr. Knowitall?

Ben: (gives his idea) **Recently**, I have **come across** a story about mermaids. I would be happy to share with you what I learned.

Stephen: Do you **believe** in mermaids? A mermaid is a creature from the **tales**.

Ben: Yes, Stephen it maybe a tale but it is part of our culture and we can learn something important from a tale, can't we?

Ming: Chinese culture and literature has many such tales,too, and our **parents** use them to teach us important lessons about good lifestyles.

Stephen: (embarrassed) Folks, do not **misunderstand** my **comment**. I **have nothing against** tales and legends. I **just** thought we are too old for tales.

Ben: Don't worry, Stephen, I did not misunderstand your comment.

Mr. Knowitall: Ok, then. Why don't we **listen** to what Ben has read about the mermaids?

Ben: (happy to share his story) A mermaid, **according to** the legend, is half woman and half fish. **Through** years people have written stories about mermaids. They **describe** mermaids as beautiful half woman and half fish who live in the sea. These creatures are described as having long, **golden hair** and beautiful singing voices. It is said that they sit on **rocks** and **comb** their long hair. When they see a man, they put a cap on his head. It is a **magic** cap. It can help the man to live **underwater** with the mermaid. The story is very old, Stephen. It may not be true but **next time** when you swim in the sea and hear a beautiful singing voice, **perhaps,**

you may see a mermaid. She is a very interesting creature and you can tell us about her. (Everybody laughs)

Mr. Knowitall: We learned so many new things about mermaids today. I am **looking forward** to learning more about legends from differenty countries when you start collecting information for our new project during the semester break. **Until then**, I wish you all a good day.

Practice Your Knowledge

Exercise #1—Vocabulary study

Task 1—Check the meaning of the following words in your dictionary. Copy the definitions.

Task 2—Find the sentence with the same word from the text and copy it or write your own sentence. Follow the example with the word **"creature"**:

Definition—a living being

Sentence—There are amazing creatures that live underwater.

❑ supplemental
Definition . . . .
. . . .
Sentence . . . .
. . . .

❑ continue
Definition . . . .
. . . .
Sentence . . . .
. . . .

❑ legend(s)
Definition . . . .
. . . .
Sentence . . . .
. . . .

❏ related to
Definition . . . .
. . . .
Sentence . . . .
. . . .

❏ compare
Definition . . . .
. . . .
Sentence . . . .
. . . .

❏ contrast
Definition . . . .
. . . .
Sentence . . . .
. . . .

❏ folks
Definition . . . .
. . . .
Sentence . . . .
. . . .

❏ the same
Definition . . . .
. . . .
Sentence . . . .
. . . .

❏ mermaids
Definition . . . .
. . . .
Sentence . . . .
. . . .

❏ ocean
Definition . . . .
. . . .
Sentence . . . .
. . . .

❑ handsome
Definition . . . .
. . . .
Sentence . . . .
. . . .
❑ similarities
Definition . . . .
. . . .
Sentence . . . .
. . . .
❑ differences
Definition . . . .
. . . .
Sentence . . . .
. . . .
❑ to sound
Definition . . . .
. . . .
Sentence . . . .
. . . .
❑ called
Definition . . . .
. . . .
Sentence . . . .
. . . .
❑ never
Definition . . . .
. . . .
Sentence . . . .
. . . .
❑ theme
Definition . . . .
. . . .
Sentence . . . .
. . . .

❑ however
Definition . . . .
. . . .
Sentence . . . .
. . . .
❑ intrigued
Definition . . . .
. . . .
Sentence . . . .
. . . .
❑ proposal
Definition . . . .
. . . .
Sentence . . . .
. . . .
❑ maybe
Definition . . . .
. . . .
Sentence . . . .
. . . .
❑ perhaps
Definition . . . .
. . . .
Sentence . . . .
. . . .
❑ project
Definition . . . .
. . . .
Sentence . . . .
. . . .
❑ collect
Definition . . . .
. . . .
Sentence . . . .
. . . .

❏ then
Definition . . . .
. . . .
Sentence . . . .
. . . .
❏ them
Definition . . . .
. . . .
Sentence . . . .
. . . .
❏ busy
Definition . . . .
. . . .
Sentence . . . .
. . . .
❏ during
Definition . . . .
. . . .
Sentence . . . .
. . . .
❏ month(s)
Definition . . . .
. . . .
Sentence . . . .
. . . .
❏ time
Definition . . . .
. . . .
Sentence . . . .
. . . .
❏ later
Definition . . . .
. . . .
Sentence . . . .
. . . .

❑ meanwhile

Definition . . . .

. . . .

Sentence . . . .

. . . .

❑ hear

Definition . . . .

. . . .

Sentence . . . .

. . . .

❑ listen

Definition . . . .

. . . .

Sentence . . . .

. . . .

❑ recently

Definition . . . .

. . . .

Sentence . . . .

. . . .

❑ believe

Definition . . . .

. . . .

Sentence . . . .

. . . .

❑ tale(s)

Definition . . . .

. . . .

Sentence . . . .

. . . .

❑ parent(s)

Definition . . . .

. . . .

Sentence . . . .

. . . .

❏ misunderstand
Definition . . . .
. . . .
Sentence . . . .
. . . .

❏ comment(s)
Definition . . . .
. . . .
Sentence . . . .
. . . .

❏ just
Definition . . . .
. . . .
Sentence . . . .
. . . .

❏ through
Definition . . . .
. . . .
Sentence . . . .
. . . .

❏ describe
Definition . . . .
. . . .
Sentence . . . .
. . . .

❏ golden
Definition . . . .
. . . .
Sentence . . . .
. . . .

❏ hair
Definition . . . .
. . . .
Sentence . . . .
. . . .

❑ rock(s)
Definition . . . .
. . . .
Sentence . . . .
. . . .
❑ comb
Definition . . . .
. . . .
Sentence . . . .
. . . .
❑ magic
Definition . . . .
. . . .
Sentence . . . .
. . . .
❑ underwater
Definition . . . .
. . . .
Sentence . . . .
. . . .

Exercise #2—Answer the following questions:

- What is a mermaid and where does she live? _____
  _____
- What does she look like? Describe the mermaid _____
  _____
- Where does she sit when she gets out of water and what does she do?
  _____
- Does she have a beautiful voice? Why does she need a beautiful voice?
  _____
- What does she put on a man's head when she falls in love with him?
  _____
- Why does she put a magical hat on the man's hat? _____
  _____

B

Exercise #3—Find the secret word and write a sentence with it.

• erercaut_____ . . . .
. . . .
. . . .
. . . .

• alustneplepm_____ . . . .
. . . .
. . . .
. . . .

• eudgirtin_____ . . . .
. . . .
. . . .
. . . .

• awretnuedr_____ . . . .
. . . .
. . . .
. . . .

• nudersimdnast_____ . . . .
. . . .
. . . .
. . . .

Exercise #4: **VOCABULARY BUILDING**—Insert the right word from the list in the blanks in the following sentences. Sentences are taken from the lesson "Mermaids".

continue	compare	contrast	describe	collect
similarities	never	golden	proposal	month
meanwhile	comment	recently	mermaid	during

• These creatures are described as having long, _____ hair and beautiful singing voices.
• They _____ mermaids as beautiful half woman and half fish who live in the sea.

- Folks, do not misundertstand my _____.
- _____, can we hear something about one of these sea creatures?
- _____, I have come across a story about mermaids.
- I like that idea but, like Monique, I have final exams this _____.
- Can we do that _____ our semester break?
- However, I am very intrigued by Carol's _____ about comparing legends from different countries.
- Maybe we can start a project to _____ legends from different countries and then compare them.
- She talks about _____ and _____and something called Venn Diagram.
- I have _____ understood what that is.
- It would be a good idea to compare your legend with our legend and see the _____ and the difference that our stories contain.
- When we were children, we were told stories about _____ that come from the ocean and fall in love with handsome guys.
- So, Mr. Knowitall has decided to _____talking about some legends related to the sea.

Exercise #5: VOCABULARY BUILDING—Use the words you learned in the lesson "Mermaids" in a new context. Make the necessary changes.

through	comment	recently	mermaid	during
continue	compare	contrast	describe	collect
similarities	never	rock	proposal	golden

- The famous painter was looking at the _____ sunset at the beach.
- I liked her _____ to collect poems but I am too busy to work on it this month.
- The mermaid sits on a _____ and starts singing to the handsome guy.
- I have _____ been to a wedding party where the bride sings to the groom.

- There are many_____ in the legends of different cultures.
- As we were driving up the mountain, we went _____ a beautiful forest.
- The student was embarrassed by his teacher's _____ on his essay.
- _____, I have visited the museum in my town.
- I had never heard stories about _____ before Mr. Knowitall taught this lesson to us.
- I go to visit my grandmother in the farm _____ my summer holidays.
- The loud noise _____ until we complained to the neighbor.
- I cannot _____ the beauty of the mountains to the beauty of the beach because they are very different.
- There is a huge _____ between the East and the West Coast weather.
- My brother likes to _____ postage stamps.
- It is difficult to _____ a mother's love for her children.

Grammar Point—Personal Pronouns: Personal pronouns take the place of a noun and they are of two kinds: Subject Pronouns and Object Pronouns.

SUBJECT PRONOUNS	OBJECT PRONOUNS
I	. . . . me
You	. . . . you
He	. . . . him
She	. . . . her

It	⟶	. . . . it
We	⟶	. . . . us
You	⟶	. . . . You
They	⟶	. . . . Them

Exercise #6—Use the correct form of the pronouns (subject or object) to complete the following sentences:

1. The mother said to her daughter: "Bring_____ (he) some oranges, please."
2. When John went to buy a present for his wife, he knew that the painting was an excellent present for _____(she).
3. "Do _____(you) want to come with _____(I) to the beach?"—asked the handsome man.
4. "I am going to visit _____(they) this summer"—promised the young girl.
5. The teacher was surprised that both final exams were the same and she asked the excellent student, "Is this the way to help _____(she)?"
6. My mother is going to meet _____(they) when they arrive at the airport.
7. I saw _____(she) at the movies with her handsome boyfriend.
8. "It is too hard to find _____(it) ", complained the little girl.
9. Bob is planning to write to _____(she) tomorrow about the death of her good friend.
10. The teacher talked to _____(he) today about the project he will finish during summer break.

—Find and fix the mistakes in the following sentences. Some pronouns are in subject case and some are in object case:

1. The mother told he _____ to feed the cat.
2. Him _____ does not know how to play soccer with she _____.
3. Them _____ are going to see she _____ in the hospital.
4. The teacher asked I _____ to do the homework more carefully.
5. Us _____ want they _____ to play with she _____.
6. Them _____ went to the movies with he _____ yesterday.
7. Us _____ want to learn English with she _____.
8. Her _____ told they _____ to be quiet because the baby was sleeping.
9. The father is teaching he _____ how to ride a bicycle but him ____ does not have the skills.
10. Him _____ is in love with she _____.

Supplemental Reading—Choose the best tittle for the following short story: a) Hundreds of Insects; b) Interesting Insects ; c) How Insects Help Us; d) How Insects Hurt Us;

Although there seem to be countless stars in the sky, there are even more different kinds of insects in the world. Scientists have found more than 800,000 kinds of insects, but many scientists believe that there are as many as 4,000,000 species. Insects live nearly everywhere they can find food. It is hard to find food in the ocean, therefore very few insects are found there. The insect plays a most important part in our lives because he eats so much and in getting food, he aids man. The honey-bee is an example of a very helpful insect. There are other insects that are harmful. They bite men, like mosquitos, and destroy millions of dollars in crops each year, like grasshoppers.

SPOT THE MISTAKE—Find the mistakes and fix them. Write the correct sentence:

This insect uses poison to kill the birds . . . .

. . . .

. . . .

. . . .

. . . .

. . . .

. . . .

. . . .

. . . .

REMEMBER THIS—To avoid confusion in writing, use commas to separate words and word groups with a series of three or more. Use a comma to separate two adjectives when the word "*and*" can not be inserted between them.

DID YOU KNOW?—Canadians consume more macaroni and cheese than any other nation in the world.

LANGUAGE BANK—In this lesson you learned:

Active words	Recycled words	Passive words
1. supplemental	1. about	1. wedding(s)
2. continue	2. hope	2. party(ies)
3. legend(s)	3. topic	3. bride(s)
4. related to	4. prepare	4. groom(s)
5. compare	5. start	5. mountain(s)
6. contrast	6. excellent	6. drive
7. folks	7. concern	7. complain
8. the same	8. contain	8. beach(es)
9. mermaids	9. share	9. postage
10. ocean	10. important	10. stamp(s)
11. handsome	11. discuss	11. difficult
12. similarities	12. interesting	12. movies
13. differences	13. enjoy	13 hospital(s)
14. to sound	14. decide	14. sleeping
15. called	15. talking	15. although
16. never	16. thinking	16. countless
17. theme	17. inflatable	17. scientist(s)
18. however	18. too	18. species
19. intrigued	19. sometimes	19. therefore
20. proposal	20. lifestyle	20. play a part
21. maybe	21. embarrassed	21. to aid
22. perhaps	22. information	22. honey-bee
23. project	23. amazing	23. helpful
24. collect	24. guys	24. harmful
25. then		25. destroy
26. the		26. crops
27. bus		27. grasshopper
28. during		
29. month(s)		
30. time		

Expressions: fall in love, Venn Diagram, do not worry, at length final exams, semester break, works better, come across, have nothing

31. later
32. meanwhile
33. hear
34. listen
35. recently
36. believe
37. tale(s)
38. parent(s)
39. misunderstand
40. comment(s)
41. just
42. through
43. describe
44. golden
45. hair
46. rock(s)
47. comb
48. magic
49. underwater
50. creature

against, according to, looking forward to, until then, next time

Lesson #4—Dragons

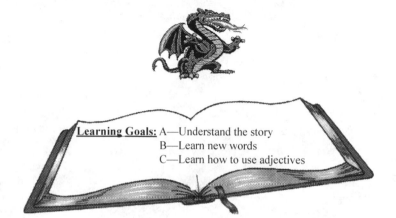

Learning Goals: A—Understand the story
B—Learn new words
C—Learn how to use adjectives

Language Structure Point: Adjectives

(Students are **interested** in learning more about different legends and **myths.** Their **interest** on the topic is helping them improve their language proficiency and Mr. Knowitall has decided to continue their discussion about legends and myths. He has prepared a **power point presentation** for his students to understand the myth of the **dragon** better.)

Mr. Knowitall: Good morning everyone. **Winter holidays are over** and now everyone in our **country** is going back to work. However, I think Ming is **getting ready** to go home to China for a very big holiday that is **celebrated** in China at the beginning of **February**, right Ming?

Ming: Yes, Mr,Knowitall. Chinese New Year is the biggest **celebration** for Chinese people and I am **planning** to go **home** for the Chinese New Year.

Mr. Knowitall: I think Chinese **folklore** is **full of** beatiful legends and **mythological** characters. **Which** character is most famous in Chinese **mythology**, Ming?

Ming: Chinese folklore **is rich in** characters but the most famous, of course, is the character of the dragon. In Chinese folklore the dragon is **considered** to be strong and **smart**. He always does good things for the people.

Ben: We have dragons in our folklore, too. They are the most resilient characters in our legends.

Carol: In our folklore, dragons have **magic** skills. They are famous for helping good people and punishing the **villains.**
George: It is amazing how different cultures share many legends.

Mr. Knowitall: That is **exactly** what I was thinking, George. **Obviously**, people from different cultures have been communicating **through ages**.

Monique: I have read some research that analyzes **facts** that have puzzled researchers through ages. That reasearch found that people have been communicating with **each** **other** through ages, **long before** the time of telephone, internet and e-mail **messages**.

Paolo: (politely disarees) Oh, Monique, the **digital age** cannot be compared to **times** when people used **seashells** to **call** each other.

Stephen: (explains) Yes, Paolo, times have **changed** but, the point Monique is trying to make is that even in **ancient** times people have found ways to communicate with each other.

Paolo: Yes, you are right, Stephen. However, **social media** today has become an amazing tool and people are using it for many **purposes**.

Carol: Yes, Paolo, but sometimes (**ironically**) your social media can become a big concern and does a lot of **harm, especially** to **young** people. So, we have to be careful and use it to help, not to harm us.

Paolo: (reluctantly agrees) You are right, Carol. I have read some facts about how some villains use social media to harm people and that is really a big concern.

George: Can we go back to our topic about myths and how different **cultures** share a number of myths and legends.

Ben: Legends about dragons intrigue me a lot. I would be very interested in hearing Ming share more information about dragon legends in Chinese culture.

Mr. Knowitall: I think that is a great idea. Ming, can you share some information about dragon legends in your folklore?

Ming: (excited) I would be happy to but I would need somebody to help me read the information I have **gathered.**

Monique: I would be glad to be your reading **partner,** Ming.

Ming: (gives Monique a written paper to read) Thanks, Monique. Here is the story: (starts reading) Many legends talk about big dragons. People **believe** that these **huge** creatures are **real**. In some legends they are described as **terrible** creatures, in some other stories they are **wonderful** creatures. They **kill** villains or they help **poor** people.

Monique: (starts reading) In different countries they are described as **large** **lizard** **beasts**. Most myths speak of them as **dangerous** beasts that live in dark **caves**. Some countries describe them as helpful because they **guard** the treasures found in those caves.

Ming: Anyone who killed the strong dragon would take the treasure. The legends talk about **brave** men who killed the terrible dragons and became famous **heroes**. Some countries have legends of wonderful dragons that help the poor people. In those myths dragons give the people all the treasure from the cave.

Mr. Knowitall: You make me proud with the ways you are improving your language skills everyday. Also, I am amazed at your level of **maturity** and the way you analyze different topics. Thank you for your hard work. Let us start working with the excercises now.

Practice Your Knowledge

Exercise #1—Vocabulary study
Task 1—Check the meaning of the following words in your dictionary. Copy the definitions.
Task 2—Find the sentence with the same word from the text and copy it or write your own sentence. Follow the example with the word **"myth"**:
   Definition—legend
   Sentence—My grandmother knows many myths and I love to listen to her stories when I visit her in summer.

❑ interested
Definition . . . .
. . . .
Sentence . . . .
. . . .

❑ myth(s)
Definition . . . .
. . . .
Sentence . . . .
. . . .
❑ interest(s)
Definition . . . .
. . . .
Sentence . . . .
. . . .
❑ power point
Definition . . . .
. . . .
Sentence . . . .
. . . .
❑ presentation(s)
Definition . . . .
. . . .
Sentence . . . .
. . . .
❑ dragon(s)
Definition . . . .
. . . .
Sentence . . . .
. . . .
❑ holiday(s)
Definition . . . .
. . . .
Sentence . . . .
. . . .
❑ country(ies)
Definition . . . .
. . . .
Sentence . . . .
. . . .

❏ celebrate
Definition . . . .
. . . .
Sentence . . . .
. . . .
❏ February
Definition . . . .
. . . .
Sentence . . . .
. . . .
❏ folklore
Definition . . . .
. . . .
Sentence . . . .
. . . .
❏ mythological
Definition . . . .
. . . .
Sentence . . . .
. . . .
❏ which
Definition . . . .
. . . .
Sentence . . . .
. . . .
❏ consider
Definition . . . .
. . . .
Sentence . . . .
. . . .
❏ smart
Definition . . . .
. . . .
Sentence . . . .
. . . .

❑ magic

Definition . . . .
. . . .

Sentence . . . .
. . . .

❑ villain(s)

Definition . . . .
. . . .

Sentence . . . .
. . . .

❑ exactly

Definition . . . .
. . . .

Sentence . . . .
. . . .

❑ obviously

Definition . . . .
. . . .

Sentence . . . .
. . . .

❑ fact(s)

Definition . . . .
. . . .

Sentence . . . .
. . . .

❑ message(s)

Definition . . . .
. . . .

Sentence . . . .
. . . .

❑ call

Definition . . . .
. . . .

Sentence . . . .
. . . .

❑ seashell(s)

Definition . . . .

. . . .

Sentence . . . .

. . . .

❑ change

Definition . . . .

. . . .

Sentence . . . .

. . . .

❑ times

Definition . . . .

. . . .

Sentence . . . .

. . . .

❑ ancient

Definition . . . .

. . . .

Sentence . . . .

. . . .

❑ purpose(s)

Definition . . . .

. . . .

Sentence . . . .

. . . .

❑ harm

Definition . . . .

. . . .

Sentence . . . .

. . . .

❑ especially

Definition . . . .

. . . .

Sentence . . . .

. . . .

❑ young
Definition . . . .
. . . .
Sentence . . . .
. . . .
❑ culture(s)
Definition . . . .
. . . .
Sentence . . . .
. . . .
❑ to gather
Definition . . . .
. . . .
Sentence . . . .
. . . .
❑ partner(s)
Definition . . . .
. . . .
Sentence . . . .
. . . .
❑ believe
Definition . . . .
. . . .
Sentence . . . .
. . . .
❑ huge
Definition . . . .
. . . .
Sentence . . . .
. . . .
❑ real
Definition . . . .
. . . .
Sentence . . . .
. . . .

❏ terrible
Definition . . . .
. . . .
Sentence . . . .
. . . .
❏ wonderful
Definition . . . .
. . . .
Sentence . . . .
. . . .
❏ kill
Definition . . . .
. . . .
Sentence . . . .
. . . .
❏ poor
Definition . . . .
. . . .
Sentence . . . .
. . . .
❏ large
Definition . . . .
. . . .
Sentence . . . .
. . . .
❏ lizard(s)
Definition . . . .
. . . .
Sentence . . . .
. . . .
❏ beast(s)
Definition . . . .
. . . .
Sentence . . . .
. . . .

❑ dangerous

Definition . . . .
. . . .
Sentence . . . .
. . . .

❑ cave(s)

Definition . . . .
. . . .
Sentence . . . .
. . . .

❑ guard

Definition . . . .
. . . .
Sentence . . . .
. . . .

❑ treasure

Definition . . . .
. . . .
Sentence . . . .
. . . .

❑ brave

Definition . . . .
. . . .
Sentence . . . .
. . . .

❑ terrible

Definition . . . .
. . . .
Sentence . . . .
. . . .

❑ hero(es)

Definition . . . .
. . . .
Sentence . . . .
. . . .

❑ maturity

Definition . . . .
. . . .
Sentence . . . .
. . . .

Exercise #2—Check for understanding: Read the story and answer the questions:

1. What is a dragon like?(use all the adjectives from Lesson #4 to describe a dragon) _____
   _____
   _____

2. What kinds of beasts are dragons? _____
   _____
   _____

3. What happened to the brave men who killed a dragon? _____
   _____
   _____

4. What do some countries think of dragons? _____
   _____
   _____

5. Have you read any stories about dragons? _____
   _____
   _____
   _____

6.

7. How do you imagine a dragon? _____
_____
_____

8. Which science studies dragon myths? _____
_____
_____
_____

Exercise #3—Find the secret word and write a sentence with it.

• relcutu_____ . . . .
. . . .
. . . .
. . . .

• ulfnowrde_____ . . . .
. . . .
. . . .
. . . .

• usondareg_____ . . . .
. . . .
. . . .
. . . .

• ylsvbooui_____ . . . .
. . . .
. . . .
. . . .

• alchtymoolig_____ . . . .
. . . .
. . . .
. . . .

Exercise #4: **VOCABULARY BUILDING**—Insert the right word from the list in the blanks in the following sentences. Make the necessary changes. Sentences are taken from the story "Dragons".

mythological	presentation	dragon	holiday
digital age	folklore	celebration	villain
brave	dangerous	guard	treasure
believe	cave	lizard	culture

- The legends talk about _____men who killed the terrible dragons and became famous heroes.
- In different countries they are described as large _____ beasts.
- Most stories speak of them as _____ beasts that live in dark _____.
- Some countries describe dragons as helpful because they _____ the treasures found in those caves.
- People _____ that these huge creatures are real.
- I have read some facts about how some _____ use social media and that is really a big concern.
- Oh, Monique, the _____ _____ cannot be compared to times when people used seashells to call each other.
- Chinese New Year is the biggest _____ for Chinese people and I am planning to go home for the Chinese New Year.
- Winter _____ are over and now everyone in our country is going back to work.
- Some countries have legends of wonderful _____, who help the poor people.
- They give them all the _____ from the cave.
- I think Chinese _____ is full of beatiful legends and _____ characters.
- He has prepared a power point _____ for his students to understand the dragon story better.

85

Exercise #5: VOCABULARY BUILDING—Use the words you learned in the story "Dragons" in a new context. Make the necessary changes.

guard	treasure	believe	cave	lizard
folklore	celebration	villain	brave	dangerous
mythological	presentation	dragon	holiday	digital age

- My brother, who is a university student, is writing a research paper on the _____ of our culture.
- A friend of mine took a very _____job protecting the polar bears as an endangered species.
- The teacher is taking special training to teach with the technology of the _____.
- John has fourteen days _____ every year.
- Heroes are _____ men who fight for freedom and become role models for young people.
- The little boy was drawing a big _____ that he read about in a _____ story.
- Sometimes, huge _____ are hidden in secret _____ far away from cities.
- Children _____ that Santa Claus comes through the chimney and brings presents.
- Many cultures have tales that talk about heroes and _____.
- Peter has left town to take part in the _____ of Remembrance Day in the capital.
- I worked all weekend to prepare a _____ on the folklore of my culture.
- My grandmother tells us tales about _____ creatures in ancient times.
- Our soldiers _____ our freedom night and day.

Grammar Point—**Adjectives:** an adjective is a word that describes the noun. **Comparative Degree**—When we compare two things or people we look at what makes them different from each other. An adjective is a word that describes the noun that follows it. It has 3 degrees: Positive, Comparative (compare two things) and Superlative (compare one thing to the whole group). Comparative degree of adjectives is used to show what quality one thing has more or less than the other. *For example:*

The man on the left is taller than the man on the right.

A car is faster than a bicycle.

The red bag is bigger than the blue bag.

The changes in different degrees depend on the length of the adjective, e.x.:

Kind of Adjective	Positive Degree	Comparative Degree	Superlative Degree
Short	tall	tall+er than	the tall+est of . . . .
	small	small+er than	the small+est of . . . .
	fine	fine+r than	the fine-st of . . . .
Long	terrible	more terrible than	the most terrible of . . . .
	dangerous	more dangerous than.	the most dangerous of
	helpful	more helpful than	the most helpful of . . .

	famous	more famous than	the most famous of . . .
Irregular	good	better than	the best of . . . .
	bad	worse than	the worst of . . . .
	many, much	more than . . .	the most . . .
	little	less more	the least of . . . .

EXAMPLES OF IRREGULAR ADJECTIVES

Adjective	Comparative	Superlative	Example
bad	worse	the worst	Historians say that the tsunami of 2004 is worse than a tornado. It is the worst disaster the world has ever seen.
far	further	the furthest	Mars is further from the Sun than Earth. Pluto is the furthest world from the Sun
good	better	the best	Her English was better than her brother's. She was the best student in the English class.
old (age)	elder	the eldest	My elder sister Karen is elder than me. She is the eldest in our family.

Exercise #6—Use the correct form adjectives to complete these sentences. Make the necessary changes.

- Her hair is _____ (long) than mine.
- A dragon is _____ (dangerous) of all beasts.
- Are you _____ (tall) your brother?
- Rabbit's ears are _____ (long) the dog's ears.
- Jacky Chen is _____ (famous) Chinese actor in the world.

- Your room is so_____ (dark). Why don't you turn the light on?
- He is _____ (good) tennis player in China.
- Sahara desert is _____ (famous) desert in Africa.
- Which river is _____ (long) in Africa?
- Which country is _____ (large) in the world?

Homework—Use the correct form of adjectives to complete these sentences. Make the necessary changes.

- His arms are _____(strong) than mine because he exercises every day.
- A dragon is _____(dangerous) of all beasts in the legends.
- Are you _____ (tall) your elder brother who goes to university?
- Donkey's ears are _____(long) the cat's ears.
- Nelson Mandela is _____(famous) freedom fighter in Africa.
- Your room is so_____ (small). Why don't you move to a new apartment?
- He is _____ (good) student in his high school.

Supplemental Reading—Choose the best tittle for the following short story: a) The Many Uses of Sharks; b) Sharks; c) Fish of Many Kinds; d) The Largest Shark;

One of the greediest eaters among the sea animals is the shark. Sharks live in all parts of the sea but they seem to prefer warm areas. They may grow to be over 40 feet long. Their bodies are covered with scales which give the skin a rough feeling much like sandpaper. Although many sharks have long rows of sharp teeth, others have broad, flat teeth. Sharks can swim rapidly and may follow ships for long days waiting for food to be thrown overboard. The largest shark, whale shark, is harmless to man. The name "whale shark" comes from the fish's physiology, being as large as many whales and also it eats plankton like many whale species. It is often over 50 feet long but feeds only on small sea animals and plants. This is the largest known fish. The whale, which is larger, is not a fish. It is a mammal. Sharks are used by man for making glue, fertilizer, cod-liver oil, leather and food.

STUDY TIP—Give yourself plenty of time to prepare for exams. Cramming doesn't work. When you start to study weeks ahead you have plenty of time to read everything. It, also, gives you time to ask questions about anything you don't fully understand.

SPOT THE MISTAKE—Find the mistakes and fix them. Write the correct sentence:

This shark lives in the Arctic Circle and eats fish. . . . .

. . . .
. . . .
. . . .
. . . .
. . . .
. . . .
. . . .

REMEMBER THIS—Coordinating conjunctions are easy to remember with a mnemonic device—**FANBOYS**: **F**or, **A**nd, **N**or, **B**ut, **O**r, **Y**et, **S**o

DID YOU KNOW?—Out of all the fish caught in the world, about three quarters are eaten as food. The other quarter is used to make such things as glue, soap, margarine, pet food and fertilizer.

LANGUAGE BANK—In this lesson you learned:

Active words	Recycled words	Passive words
1. interested	1. different	1. university(ies)
2. myth(s)	2. legend(s)	2. research
3. interest(s)	3. topic(s)	3. endagared
4. power point	4. help	4. polar bear(s)
5. presentation	5. improve	5. training
6. dragon	6. language(s)	6. freedom
7. winter	7. proficiency	7. role model(s)
8. holiday(s)	8. decide	8. Santa Claus
9. country(ies)	9. continue	9. chimney(ies)
10. celebrate	10. discussion(s)	10. capital(s)
11. February	11. prepare	11. take part
12. folklore	12. understand	12. Remembrance Day
13. mythological	13. character(s)	13. weekend(s)
14. which	14. famous	14. soldier(s)
15. consider	15. resilient	15 adjective(s)
16. smart	16. amazing	16. quality(ies)
17. magic	17. communicate	17. left
18. villain(s)	18. analyze	18. historian(s)
19. exactly	19. research	19. dictator(s)
20. obviously	20. researcher(s)	20. shark(s)
21. fact(s)	21. puzzled	21. greedy
22. message(s)	22. point	22. killer
23. call	23. way(s)	23. prefer
24. seashell(s)	24. today	24. grow
25. change	25. become	25. scale(s)
26. times	26. concern(s)	26. rough
27. ancient	27. reluctantly	
28. purpose(s)	28. agree	
29. harm	29. to intrigue	

30. especially
31. young
32. culture(s)
33. to gather
34. partner(s)
35. believe
36. huge
37. real
38. terrible
39. wonderful
40. kill
41. poor
42. large
43. lizard(s)
44. beast(s)
45. dangerous
46. cave(s)
47. guard
48. treasure
49. brave
50. terrible
51. hero(es)
52. maturity

30. interested
31. describe
32. creature(s)

Expressions: are over, getting ready, full of, through ages, each other long before, digital age, social media

Lesson #5—Active Living or Couch Potato?

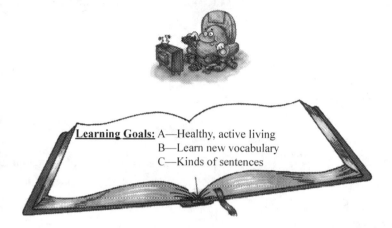

Learning Goals: A—Healthy, active living
B—Learn new vocabulary
C—Kinds of sentences

Language Structure Point: Declarative, Negative, Interrogative Sentences

(Mr. Knowitall and his students have **already** talked about their healthy lifestyles. Now they are analyzing a lifestyle that does not help people stay healthy. They will also talk about how young people can play healthy games and **fight obesity instead of** becoming a **couch potato**.)

Mr. Knowitall: Today we will consider an interesting problem that we have discussed before—healthy lifestyles.

Ben: (**shares**) I have written a story about my wonderful neighbours and my friends and I will read it to you. I will start—Mrs. Brown is my wonderful neighbor. Her **favorite** sport is **swimming**. She goes to the **swimming pool** every day.

Carol (**keeps** telling the story) She **likes** playing tennis, **also**. She usually plays tennis with my mother on weekend.

George: Like most women, Mrs. Brown likes **to shop**, also. She goes shopping to the shopping mall.

Monique: Her favorite shops are those that sell shoes and **scarves**.

Paolo: Sometimes, she **has lunch** at the Chinese **restaurant** near the **shopping mall** so she can **take a break** and then **continue** shopping.

Ming: It is great that she eats Chinese food because it is healthy and **nutritious**.

Stephen: (continues to read) Mrs. Brown is married to Mr. Brown. He is her **husband**; however, he is a very different **person**.

Ming: How is her husband different from his **wife**?

Ben: His lifestyle is very different from his wife's; he does not like swimming or playing games. He does not go to the swimming pool or for walks.

Carol: His **hobby** is **soccer**. However, he reluctantly ever plays soccer. He is interested only in **watching** the **match** on TV. He sits and plays computer games all the time. He is a couch potato.

Mr. Knowitall: This is an interesting story. There is a number of people who are living very **passive** lifestyles. That is **becoming** a very **serious** problem especially with school children.

Ming: Yes, that is a serious problem in our school, too. Watching television and playing computer games causes obesity. Obesity is obviously caused by the passive lifestyle.

George: I am sorry **to interrupt** but I do not understand the word "obesity". Can somebody explain it to me, please?

Monique: The **concept** of obesity has intrigued me for a long time and have done some research. Here is what I found: The World Health Organization (WHO) says—Overweight and obesity are **defined** as **abnormal** or **excessive** fat **accumulation** that presents a **risk** to a person's health.

Paolo: That obviously is a problem with me as I sit at the computer for hours. I need to change that passive lifestyle, get out and play sports more in the future or I will become a couch potato.

Stephen: I am very impressed with your maturity level, Paolo. If you want, you can play soccer every Friday afternoon with my team.

Ming: I would be happy to teach you how to play Kong Fu, Paolo.

Paolo:Thanks a lot my friends. I will **join** both of you in your **active** lifestyles.

Mr. Knowitall: That is a wonderful idea. Our health is our treasure and we need to guard it through our active lifestyle. Living like a couch potato is dangerous and we need to be resilient in choosing the best ways to **exercise** **regularly**. Thanks for your wonderful ideas on this topic.

Practice Your Knowledge

Exercise **#1**—Vocabulary study
Task 1—Check the meaning of the following words in your dictionary. Copy the definitions.

Task 2—Find the sentence with the same word from the text and copy it or write your own sentence. Follow the example with the word **"neighbor"**:

Definition—somebody who lives nearby
Sentence—I have a very good neighbor.

❏ favorite
Definition . . . .
. . . .
Sentence . . . .
. . . .

❏ share
Definition . . . .
. . . .
Sentence . . . .
. . . .

❏ sport
Definition . . . .
. . . .
Sentence . . . .
. . . .

❏ swim
Definition . . . .
. . . .
Sentence . . . .
. . . .

❏ swimming pool
Definition . . . .
. . . .
Sentence . . . .
. . . .

❏ every day
Definition . . . .
. . . .
Sentence . . . .
. . . .

❏ tennis
Definition . . . .
. . . .
Sentence . . . .
. . . .
❏ usually
Definition . . . .
. . . .
Sentence . . . .
. . . .
❏ shop
Definition . . . .
. . . .
Sentence . . . .
. . . .
❏ shopping mall
Definition . . . .
. . . .
Sentence . . . .
. . . .
❏ scarf(ves)
Definition . . . .
. . . .
Sentence . . . .
. . . .
❏ sometimes
Definition . . . .
. . . .
Sentence . . . .
. . . .
❏ restaurant(s)
Definition . . . .
. . . .
Sentence . . . .
. . . .

❏ near
Definition . . . .
. . . .
Sentence . . . .
. . . .

❏ married
Definition . . . .
. . . .
Sentence . . . .
. . . .

❏ hobby(ies)
Definition . . . .
. . . .
Sentence . . . .
. . . .

❏ soccer
Definition . . . .
. . . .
Sentence . . . .
. . . .

❏ to watch
Definition . . . .
. . . .
Sentence . . . .
. . . .

❏ the match(es)
Definition . . . .
. . . .
Sentence . . . .
. . . .

❏ wife(ves)
Definition . . . .
. . . .
Sentence . . . .
. . . .

❏ game(s)
Definition . . . .
. . . .
Sentence . . . .
. . . .
❏ risk(s)
Definition . . . .
. . . .
Sentence . . . .
. . . .
❏ active
Definition . . . .
. . . .
Sentence . . . .
. . . .
❏ keep
Definition . . . .
. . . .
Sentence . . . .
. . . .
❏ to exercise
Definition . . . .
. . . .
Sentence . . . .
. . . .
❏ regularly
Definition . . . .
. . . .
Sentence . . . .
. . . .
❏ already
Definition . . . .
. . . .
Sentence . . . .
. . . .

❏ fight
Definition . . . .
. . . .
Sentence . . . .
. . . .
❏ obesity
Definition . . . .
. . . .
Sentence . . . .
. . . .
❏ also
Definition . . . .
. . . .
Sentence . . . .
. . . .
❏ nutritious
Definition . . . .
. . . .
Sentence . . . .
. . . .
❏ husband
Definition . . . .
. . . .
Sentence . . . .
. . . .
❏ person
Definition . . . .
. . . .
Sentence . . . .
. . . .
❏ passive
Definition . . . .
. . . .
Sentence . . . .
. . . .

❑ become

Definition . . . .
. . . .
Sentence . . . .
. . . .

❑ serious

Definition . . . .
. . . .
Sentence . . . .
. . . .

❑ interrupt

Definition . . . .
. . . .
Sentence . . . .
. . . .

❑ concept

Definition . . . .
. . . .
Sentence . . . .
. . . .

❑ define

Definition . . . .
. . . .
Sentence . . . .
. . . .

❑ abnormal

Definition . . . .
. . . .
Sentence . . . .
. . . .

❑ excessive

Definition . . . .
. . . .
Sentence . . . .
. . . .

❏ accumulation

Definition . . . .
. . . .
Sentence . . . .
. . . .

Exercise #2—Check for understanding: Read the story and answer the questions.

1. Who is Mrs. Brown? _____

2. What does she do every day? _____

3. Who is Mr. Brown? _____

4. What does he like to do in his free time? _____

5. Does Mr. Brown like to go shopping? _____

6. What is a "couch potato"? _____

7. What problems can obesity cause? _____

8. How can a person become active and healthy? _____

9. What is a healthy and active lifestyle? _____

10. What did you learn from this story? _____

Exercise #3—Find the secret word and write a sentence with it.

• soutiirtnu _____ . . . .
. . . .
. . . .

• malnorab _____ . . . .
. . . .
. . . .

• voafriet _____ . . . .
. . . .
. . . .

• eruastratn _____ . . . .
. . . .
. . . .

• cacuumaltion _____ . . . .
. . . .
. . . .

• boiesyt _____ . . . .
. . . .
. . . .

Exercise #4: **VOCABULARY BUILDING**—Insert the right word from the list in the blanks in the following sentences. Sentences are taken from the story "Active Living or Couch Potato?".

restaurant	hobby	already	soccer
obesity	nutritious	husband	define
excessive	passive	abnormal	accumulation

1. Overweight and obesity are _____ as _____ or _____ fat _____ that presents a risk to a person's health.

2. _____ is obviously caused by the passive lifestyle.

3. His _____ is soccer.

4. If you want, you can play _____ every Friday afternoon with my team.
5. Mr. Knowitall and his students have _____ talked about their healthy lifestyles.
6. Sometimes, she has lunch at the Chinese _____ near the shopping mall so she can take a break and then continue shopping.
7. It is great that she eats Chinese food because it is healthy and _____.
8. He is her _____; however, he is a very different person.
9. I need to change that _____ lifestyle and get out and play sports more in the future.

Exercise #5: VOCABULARY BUILDING—Use the words you learned in the story "Active Living or Couch Potato?" in a new context:

obesity	nutritious	husband	define
excessive	passive	abnormal	accumulation
restaurant	hobby	already	soccer

1. He is sick today and cannot to school because of _____ drinking at the party.
2. Every Monday night my family goes to a _____ in the neighborhood.
3. I like dancing; it is my _____ and it helps my active living style.
4. My friend, Jim, plays computer games all day and that is his _____ lifestyle.
5. He ate a whole pizza for dinner and this is quite _____.
6. Her obesity is _____ the cause of her diabetes but she keeps her lifestyle.
7. The _____ of all these games has become my brother's hobby.
8. The most popular game in Europe is _____.
9. Her desire to eating junk food is causing serious _____ concerns.
10. My mother is very concerned about our health and she always cooks _____ food.

11. The relationship between _____ and wife _____
    the children's future.

Grammar Point—Affirmative, Negative, and Interrogative sentences:

Affirmative sentences are telling sentences, they tell something. We put a period (.) at the end of an affirmative sentence. We use the formula(S+V+O) **Subject** + **Verb** (Predicate) + **Object** e. x.: I am a student.

Negative sentences are sentences that tell us that something is not true. We use the verb **"do not"** or **"does not"** to form negative sentences. e. x.: I **do not (don't)** speak Japanese. **REMEMBER**—in formal writing we do not use the short form "don't" or "doesn't".

Interrogative sentences are asking sentences, questions. We put a question mark (?) at the end of an interrogative sentence. To form an interrogative sentence, we put **"do"** or **"does"** before the subject of the affirmative sentence. e. x.: Do you like oranges?

Exercise #6—Change the sentence into the correct form. Follow this example: He goes to university. (This is a declarative sentence.) Change it into an Interrogative sentence—Does he go to university?

❑ She studies English at school. (This is a/an—sentence.)
Change it into an Interrogative sentence _____
_____

❑ He does not play soccer. (This is a/an—sentence.)
Change it into an Affirmative sentence _____
_____

❑ Does she read every day? (This is a/an—sentence.)
Change it into an Affirmative sentence _____
_____

❑ Does she speak English at home? (This is a/an—sentence.)
Change it into a Negative sentence _____

❑ Do you like swimming? (This is a/an—sentence.)
Change it into a Declarative sentence _____

_____

Homework—Follow the directions and make the necessary changes.

1. Make the sentence interrogative: You have worked for me before.....
....

2. Make the sentence negative: I have this document.................
....

3. Make the sentence an affirmative: I did not promise to increase your salary...

4. Make the sentence negative: I finished my work....................
....

5. Make the sentence affirmative: Did you finish your work?.........
....

6. Make the sentence interrogative: You gave me the money.........
....

7. Make the sentence negative: I can do this work....................
....

8. Make the sentence affirmative: I have not collected all necessary certificates...

9. Make the sentence interrogative: The work in the factory is hard.....
....

10. Make the sentence negative: I can speak German.................
....

Supplemental Reading—Choose the best tittle for this newspaper article: a) The U.S Joins Soccer; b) American Soccer Teams; c) Soccer—A Popular Sport; d) Learning to Play Soccer;

Many people claim that soccer is the most popular sport in the world. One hundred and forty-two nations belong to Soccer International

Federation. Other nations, also, play the game but do not enter international competition. Every four years the best national soccer teams in the world gather for almost a month to compete for the World Cup. In 1974, sixteen teams competed for the Cup. The defending champion, Brazil, competed against the host nation, Germany and fourteen other countries. The United States that has not been competitive in this sport, failed to qualify for the World Cup. In the championship game the strong defensive team of Germany met the strong offensive team of The Netherlands. The German team was victorious and won the World Cup.

Study **STUDY TIP**—**When learning a language, first understand others, then attempt to be understood**—When you are learning (words, a story, etc.) ask the teacher's opinion. Then ask yourself how you can best use that word in a new situation.

SPOT THE MISTAKE—Find the mistakes and fix them. Write the correct sentence:

This wife   lives a very active lifestyle . . . .
. . . .
. . . .
. . . .
. . . .
. . . .
. . . .

REMEMBER THIS—June 11 is National Get Outdoors Day (GO Day). Go Day encourages kids and families to go outside, get moving, and explore forests and parks. The best part—it's FREE!

DID YOU KNOW?—1 in 3 kids is considered overweight or obese in the U.S. Take some healthy, positive steps to help your whole family get active, eat well, prevent obesity and the diseases associated with it.

LANGUAGE BANK—In this lesson you learned:

Active words	Recycled words	Passive words
1. favorite	1. parent(s)	1. step(s)
2. share	2. brush(es)	2. obese
3. sport	3. different	3. prevent
4. swim	4. healthy	4. associated
5. swimming pool	5. lifestyle(s)	5. popular
6. every day	6. interesting	6. join
7. tennis	7. consider	7. claim
8. usually	8. wonderful	8. world
9. shop	9. analyze	9. nation(s)
10. shopping mall	10. sometimes	10. federation(s)
11. scarf(ves)	11. however	11. competition(s)
12. restaurant(s)	12. reluvtantly	12. enter
13. near	13. continue	13. almost
14. married	14. especially	14. compete
15. hobby(ies)	15. obviously	15. host
16. soccer	16. intrigued	16. competitive
17. watch	17. research	17. qualify
18. match	18. treasure	18. championship(s)
19. wife(ves)	19. protect	19. defensive
20. game(s)	20. guard	20. offensive
21. risk	21. dangerous	21. victorious
22. active	22. resilient	
23. keep	23. way(s)	

24. toexercise
25. regularly
26. already
27. fight
28. obesity
29. also
30. nutritious
31. husband
32. person
33. passive
34. become
35. serious
36. interrupt
37. concept
38. define
39. abnormal
40. excessive
41. accumulation

24. topic

Expressions: couch potato, instead of, have lunch, take a break

Lesson #6—At the Restaurant

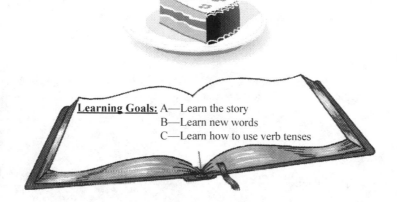

Learning Goals: A—Learn the story
B—Learn new words
C—Learn how to use verb tenses

Language Structure Point: Verb Tenses (1)

(Mr. Knowitall and his students **had dinner** at a restaurant **last night**. Different people **ordered** different **dishes**. Carol enjoyed her **dessert** very much and learned the **expression** "**to have a sweet tooth**". Today they will discuss about different situations at a restaurant and hospitality.)

Mr. Knowitall: Good morning folks. I just wanted to let you know how much I enjoyed our **dinner** last night.

Ben: Me, too. It was my first time at a Canadian restaurant and I enjoyed the **experience** very much.

Carol: (shy) At first I was very **nervous** to speak to the **waiter** because I do not speak English very well but then I **felt** very **comfortable** to order my **meal.**

George: Last week, Monique and I **invited** our friend Nick to have dinner with us in the city. We went to a very nice restaurant where there were **candles burning** in **silver candlesticks** on every table.

Monique: The place was very **elegant** and there was a **gentleman** playing the piano by the large windows which were **decorated** with nice **drapes**.

Paolo: What did you order for dinner, George?

George: I ordered **chicken** and a **tomato salad**.

Stephen: How about you, Monique?

Monique: I ordered **beef** and **fries** and some fruit.

Ming: What did your guest order?

George: Nick ordered **soup** because he wanted to **save some space** for dessert. Nick has a sweet tooth and desserts are **delicious** to have at the end of a meal.

Monique: However, George was **uncomfortable** that Nick was ordering only soup. He felt as if he was not being a good **host**.

Mr. Knowitall: Sometimes, that can be a very difficult **situation** because you want to **honour** your **guest** but you are **not sure** how to be a good host.

Ben: So, what did you guys do in that situation?

Monique: Nick **understood** our **feelings** and ordered **fish** and potatoes, too. After he finished the **food**, he was not **hungry anymore**.

George: Still, he ordered a **slice** of **cheesecake** with strawberry on **top**. He enjoyed his dessert very much and that made me so happy.

Carol: In different **cultures hospitality traditions** are very different. In my culture **for example**, the host **provides** too many kinds of dishes for the guest. Now that I have lived in Canada I understand that this tradition may make the guest uncomfortable.

George: We have **the same** tradition in my culture that is why I was uncomfortable when Nick ordered only soup.

Paolo: Some of the families in our villages are very **poor**. However, to honour the guest they will cook one of the only two chickens they may have in their little farm.

Stephen: That is **normal** in my culture, too. To describe how important the guest is, we have an expression: "The house **belongs** to God and Guest".

Ming: In Chinese culture, the guest is considered very **special**, too. One of the ways to honour the guest is by **offering** lots of food. That tradition goes back to the time when people were very poor and food was **scarce**. So, providing lots of food for the guest was considered very special and **important**.

Mr. Knowitall: All these traditions from your cultures are wonderful and I **appreciate** your **sharing** of your traditions. I **grew up** in a farm and we shared some of the traditions you described. This was a great information for all of us. Thank you, everybody.

Practice Your Knowledge

Exercise #1—Vocabulary study
Task 1—Check the meaning of the following words in your dictionary. Copy the definitions.
Task 2—Find the sentence with the same word from the text and copy it or write your own sentence. Follow the example with the word "**sound(s)**"

Definition—something that can be heard
Sentence—I listen to the sounds of birds singing in spring.

❏ dish(es)
Definition . . . .
. . . .
Sentence . . . .
. . . .

❏ dessert(s)
Definition . . . .
. . . .
Sentence . . . .
. . . .

❏ expression(s)
Definition . . . .
. . . .
Sentence . . . .
. . . .

❏ dinner(s)
Definition . . . .
. . . .
Sentence . . . .
. . . .

❏ night(s)
Definition . . . .
. . . .
Sentence . . . .
. . . .

❏ last
Definition . . . .
. . . .
Sentence . . . .
. . . .

❏ experience(s)
Definition . . . .
. . . .
Sentence . . . .
. . . .

❑ nervous
Definition . . . .
. . . .
Sentence . . . .
. . . .
❑ feel
Definition . . . .
. . . .
Sentence . . . .
. . . .
❑ comfortable
Definition . . . .
. . . .
Sentence . . . .
. . . .
❑ uncomfortable
Definition . . . .
. . . .
Sentence . . . .
. . . .
❑ meal(s)
Definition . . . .
. . . .
Sentence . . . .
. . . .
❑ invite
Definition . . . .
. . . .
Sentence . . . .
. . . .
❑ candle(s)
Definition . . . .
. . . .
Sentence . . . .
. . . .

❑ candlestick(s)
Definition . . . .
. . . .
Sentence . . . .
. . . .

❑ burn
Definition . . . .
. . . .
Sentence . . . .
. . . .

❑ silver
Definition . . . .
. . . .
Sentence . . . .
. . . .

❑ elegant
Definition . . . .
. . . .
Sentence . . . .
. . . .

❑ gentleman
Definition . . . .
. . . .
Sentence . . . .
. . . .

❑ decorate
Definition . . . .
. . . .
Sentence . . . .
. . . .

❑ drapes
Definition . . . .
. . . .
Sentence . . . .
. . . .

❏ order
Definition . . . .
. . . .
Sentence . . . .
. . . .
❏ chicken
Definition . . . .
. . . .
Sentence . . . .
. . . .
❏ tomato
Definition . . . .
. . . .
Sentence . . . .
. . . .
❏ salad
Definition . . . .
. . . .
Sentence . . . .
. . . .
❏ soup
Definition . . . .
. . . .
Sentence . . . .
. . . .
❏ delicious
Definition . . . .
. . . .
Sentence . . . .
. . . .
❏ host
Definition . . . .
. . . .
Sentence . . . .
. . . .

❑ guest
Definition . . . .
. . . .
Sentence . . . .
. . . .

❑ situation
Definition . . . .
. . . .
Sentence . . . .

❑ honour
Definition . . . .
. . . .
Sentence . . . .
. . . .

❑ understand
Definition . . . .
. . . .
Sentence . . . .

❑ feeling(s)
Definition . . . .
. . . .
Sentence . . . .
. . . .

❑ fish
Definition . . . .
. . . .
Sentence . . . .
. . . .

❑ food
Definition . . . .
. . . .
Sentence . . . .
. . . .

❑ hungry

Definition . . . .
. . . .
Sentence . . . .
. . . .

❑ anymore

Definition . . . .
. . . .
Sentence . . . .
. . . .

❑ slice

Definition . . . .
. . . .
Sentence . . . .
. . . .

❑ cheesecake

Definition . . . .
. . . .
Sentence . . . .
. . . .

❑ top

Definition . . . .
. . . .
Sentence . . . .
. . . .

❑ hospitality

Definition . . . .
. . . .
Sentence . . . .
. . . .

❑ tradition(s)

Definition . . . .
. . . .
Sentence . . . .
. . . .

❏ culture(s)
Definition . . . .
. . . .
Sentence . . . .
. . . .

❏ for example
Definition . . . .
. . . .
Sentence . . . .
. . . .

❏ provide
Definition . . . .
. . . .
Sentence . . . .
. . . .

❏ the same
Definition . . . .
. . . .
Sentence . . . .
. . . .

❏ some
Definition . . . .
. . . .
Sentence . . . .
. . . .

❏ poor
Definition . . . .
. . . .
Sentence . . . .
. . . .

❏ normal
Definition . . . .
. . . .
Sentence . . . .
. . . .

121

❏ belong

Definition . . . .

. . . .

Sentence . . . .

. . . .

❏ special

Definition . . . .

. . . .

Sentence . . . .

. . . .

❏ offer

Definition . . . .

. . . .

Sentence . . . .

. . . .

❏ scarce

Definition . . . .

. . . .

Sentence . . . .

. . . .

❏ important

Definition . . . .

. . . .

Sentence . . . .

. . . .

❏ appreciate

Definition . . . .

. . . .

Sentence . . . .

. . . .

❏ sharing

Definition . . . .

. . . .

Sentence . . . .

. . . .

Exercise #2—Check if you understood the discussion. Answer the following questions:

1. Where did Monique and George take Nick for dinner? _____
    _____

2. Describe the restaurant _____
    _____

3. What were the candlesticks made of? _____
    _____

4. What did George order for dinner? _____
    _____

5. What did Monique order for dinner? _____
    _____

6. What did Nick have for dessert and why was George uncomfortable with that? _____
    _____

7. Describe some of the best hospitality traditions in your culture
    _____
    _____

B

Exercise #3—Find the secret word and write a sentence with it.

*   papriecaet_____ . . . .
    . . . .
    . . . .

*   ateblorfomcun_____ . . . .
    . . . .
    . . . .

*   kcneihc_____ . . . .
    . . . .

*   oshipytilat _____ . . . .
    . . . .
    . . . .

- nameltneg_____ . . . .
. . . .
. . . .
- sionserpxe_____ . . . .
. . . .
. . . .
- stckieldnac_____ . . . .
. . . .
. . . .

Exercise #4: **VOCABULARY BUILDING**—Insert the right word from the list in the blanks in the following sentences. Sentences are taken from the story "At the Restaurant".

provide	hospitality	uncomfortable	important
order	candlestick	experience	dessert
expression	dish	decorated	slice
understood	hungry	tradition	belong

- Different people _____ different _____.
- To describe how _____ the guest is, we have an expression: "The house _____ to God and Guest".
- In different cultures _____ are very different.
- In my culture for example, the host _____ too many kinds of dishes for the guest.
- Carol enjoyed her_____ very much and learned the _____ "to have a sweet tooth".
- Still, he ordered a _____ of cheesecake with strawberry on top.
- Nick _____our feelings and ordered fish and potatoes, too.
- After he finished the food, he was not _____ anymore.
- We went to a very nice restaurant where there were candles burning in silver _____on every table.
- However, George was _____ that Nick was ordering only soup.

- The place was very elegant and there was a gentleman playing the piano by the large windows which were _____ with nice drapes.
- It was my first time at a Canadian restaurant and I enjoyed the _____ very much.

Exercise #5: VOCABULARY BUILDING—Use the words you learned in the story "At the Restaurant" in a new context. Make the necessary changes.

understood	hungry	tradition	belong
order	candlestick	experience	dessert
expression	dish	decorated	slice
provide	hospitality	uncomfortable	important

- It is very _____ to read in order to improve my English proficiency.
- Finally, the young man _____ the importance of living a healthy lifestyle after the doctor showed the test results.
- Jim starts his mornings with a cup of coffee and a _____ of bread that he toasts in the toaster.
- A group of friends went to the restaurant and _____ different _____.
- The English teacher shares many new _____ with her students and expects the students to use them in sentences.
- Parents are always ready to _____ help for their children.
- _____ is considered very important in many cultures.
- John had not studied for the exam and he felt very _____ because he could not answer many questions.
- Monique _____ the room with silver _____ because it was her birthday.
- My mother makes a delicious _____ with strawberries and eggs.
- This house _____ to Mrs. Brown.
- Ben came from school _____ and made a big sandwich for himself.

- I always enjoy a new _____ when talking to a person I do not know.
- Different cultures share many beautiful _____.

Grammar Point—**Verbs Tenses**—The **verb** is perhaps the most important part of the sentence. A **verb** explains something about the subject (the doer of the action) of the sentence and expresses actions, events, or states of being, for example: The mosquito **bites** people on the neck. The verb "bites" describes the action the mosquito takes. In early October, Andrew **will plant** twenty tulip bulbs. The verb "will plant" describes an action that will take place in the future.

A verb indicates the time of an action, event or condition by changing its form. Through the use of a sequence of tenses in a sentence or in a paragraph, it is possible to indicate the complex relationship of actions, events, and conditions in the sentence or paragraph. There are many ways of categorizing the twelve possible verb tenses. Verbs can be in different tense forms. They can be regular or irregular. Each sentence must have a verb.

Verb	Present (today)	Past (yesterday)	Future (tomorrow)
Regular	walk(s)	walk+ed	will walk
	work(s)	work+ed	will work
Irregular	go(es)	went	will go
	see(s)	saw	wil see

Present Tense is used when:
- we say that an action is repeated all the time, e. x.: I **brush** my teeth every morning and every evening.
- we say a general truth, e. x.: The sun **comes** up in the morning.
- we describe a number of actions which happen in the present time, e.x.: Today Ben **goes** to the market to buy some vegetables. After that he **visits** a museum and then **goes** to see his grandmother. (we use these words in sentences with verbs in the present tense—today, every day, every morning, always, at night, every year, every Sunday)

Exercise #6: Use the correct tenses of verbs to complete these sentences:

1. They _____(eat) vegetables every day.
2. She _____(speak) Chinese.
3. I _____(go) to school next week.
4. My husband _____(come) tomorrow.
5. He _____(work) in a hospital.
6. Mary and John _____(go) to Paris last summer.
7. Nick _____(walk) usually a mile a day.
8. The boy _____(brush) his teeth before going to bed.
9. It _____(rain) all day yesterday.
10. The soccer team _____(play) under a hot sun.

Exercise #7—Use the Simple Present tense to show a **repeated action** or to express the idea that an action is repeated or usual. The action can be a habit, a hobby, a daily event, a scheduled event or something that often happens.

X X X ✹ X X X
Past   Present   Future

1. I . . . . tennis every day. (to play)
2. She . . . . tennis ever.(not to play)
3. . . . . he . . . . tennis on Friday? (to play?)
4. The train . . . . every morning at 8 AM. (leave)
5. The train . . . . at 9 AM on Monday. (not to leave)
6. When . . . . the train usually . . . . ? (to leave?)
7. She always . . . . her purse in the car.(to forget)
8. He never . . . . his wallet.(to forget)

9. Every twelve months, the Earth . . . . the Sun. (to circle)
10. . . . . the Sun . . . . the Earth?(to circle?)

Exercise #8—Simple Present tense can show **Facts or Generalizations**—indicates the speaker believes that <u>a fact was true before, is true now,</u> and <u>will be true in the future</u>. It is not important if the speaker is correct about the fact.

	True	True	True
		┼	
Past		Present	Future

1. Cats . . . . milk.(to like)
2. Birds . . . . milk.(not to like)
3. . . . . pigs . . . . milk? (to like?)
4. Alberta . . . . a province of Canada.(to be)
5. Alberta . . . . in the United Kingdom. (not to be)
6. Windows . . . . made of glass. (to be)
7. Windows . . . . made of wood.(to be not)
8. Vancouver . . . . a big city. (to be)

Homework—Simple Present tense indicates **Scheduled Events in the Near Future**. This is most commonly done when talking about public transportation.

		X
Past	Present	Future

• The train . . . . tonight at 6 PM. (to leave)
• The bus . . . . .at 11:00 AM, it arrives at 11:00 PM. (not to arrive)

- When . . . . we . . . . the plane? (to board?)
- The party . . . . at 8 o'clock. (to start)
- When . . . . class . . . . tomorrow? (to begin?)

Supplemental Reading—Choose the best tittle for the following short story: a) Harmful Caterpillars; b) Catching Butterflies; c) Beautiful Insects; d) The Habits of Butterflies

Butterflies are the most beautiful of all insects. Poets have called them "winged flowers" and "flying gems". They are found throughout the world. It is hard to believe that a beautiful butterfly was once a wormlike caterpillar. Caterpillars hatch from eggs of butterflies and latter turn into butterflies. Although the caterpillar eats leaves and fruit and can harm crops, the butterfly does no harm because it cannot bite or chew. Butterflies do not grow in size as they get older. They remain the same size throughout their lifetime. No one knows why they are called butterflies. Perhaps it is because many of them are bright yellow like butter.

STUDY TIP—Learning a language is very important but it does not happen by magic. You will be expected to think for yourself almost all the time—your teachers will help you all the way but YOU will have to take control of your own learning.

SPOT THE MISTAKE—Find the mistakes and fix them. Write the correct sentence:

This wonderful and serious teacher is providing food for the children. . . . .
. . . .

. . . .
. . . .
. . . .
. . . .

 REMEMBER THIS—All **verbs**, whether regular or irregular, have five forms: the infinitive, simple present, simple past, past participle, and present participle. The difference between a regular and an irregular verb is the formation of the simple past and past participle.

DID YOU KNOW?—A cat has 32 muscles in each ear.

LANGUAGE BANK—In this lesson you learned:

Active words	Recycled words	Passive words
1. dish(es)	1. restaurant(s)	1. test(s)
2. dessert(s)	2. different	2. result(s)
3. expression(s)	3. people	3. toast
4. dinner(s)	4. enjoy	4. toaster(s)
5. night(s)	5. nice	5. finally
6. last	6. fruit	6. expect
7. experience(s)	7. difficult	7. answer(s)
8. nervous	8. potato	8. plant
9. feel	9. important	9. event(s)
10. comfortable	10. why	10. sequence(s)
11. meal(s)	11. when	11. paragraph(s)
12. invite	12. family	12. indicate
13. candle(s)	13. village	13. complex
14. candlestick(s)	14. however	14. relationship(s)
15. burn	15. little	15. categorize

16. silver
17. elegant
18. gentleman
19. decorate
20. drapes
21. order
22. chicken
23. tomato
24. salad
25. soup
26. delicious
27. uncomfortable
28. host(s)
29. guest(s)
30. situation(s)
31. honour
32. understand
33. feeling(s)
34. fish
35. hungry
36. anymore
37. slice(s)
38. cheesecake
39. top
40. hospitality
41. tradition(s)
42. culture(s)
43. for example
44. provide
45. the same
46. some
47. poor
48. belong
49. normal
50. special
51. offer
52. scarce
53. appreciate
54. sharing

16. farm
17. describe
18. house
19. consider
20. way(s)
21. food

16. commonly
17. public
18. transportation
19. wing
20. gem
21. believe
22. caterpillar
23. hatch

Expressions: to have a sweet tooth, have dinner, save some space, am not sure, grow up

Lesson #7—When the Sun Went Away

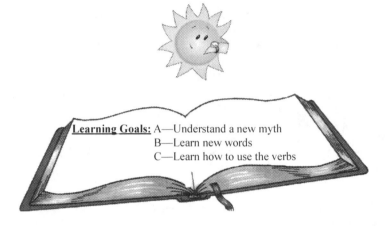

Learning Goals: A—Understand a new myth
B—Learn new words
C—Learn how to use the verbs

Language Structure Point: More About Verbs (2)

(Mr.Knowitall is **satisfied** with his students' **progress** in English but he would like to see that progress **reflected** in the **subjects** students are studying at school, like Social Studies or English Language Arts. So, today he **plans** to ask his students how they are doing in other subjects at school.)

Mr. Knowitall: (enters the classroom with a very elegant **step** like the gentleman he is) Good morning everybody. Yesterday I met your English Language Art's teacher and talked to her about your progress in her class.

Ben: Mr. Knowitall. I am feeling nervous about what my teacher may have said about my English proficiency.

Carol: Me too. I appreciate her help in class but I am very nervous to share my answers in class because in my culture you answer only if the teacher **calls** your name.

George: Come on you guys. **Show** a little **self confidence**. I feel uncomfortable when my friends make the situation look so difficult. I think we are **doing fine** in our classes.

Monique: **Usually** I am self confident but when I am in classess with my Canadian **classmates**, I am **intimidated** because I feel I am not **fluent** in English. It is an honour to come from my country but it is a big **responsibility**, too, because I **represent** my people.

Paolo: That is exactly how I feel when I speak English in class. It makes me very uncomfortable but my classmates are very **supportive**.

Stephen: Why should you feel uncomfortable, man? You already speak one and may be two other languages but it will take some time to **master academic** English.

Ming: My **teammates** are very supportive of me and they always try to **explain** the difficult words to me.

Mr. Knowitall: Folks, there is **nothing to worry about**. Your teacher **spoke very highly of** your progress in her class. She is very **proud** of you and so am I. She said you have been discussing about a Japanese legend in her class and I would like to hear what that legend is about.

Ben: Well, let me start and then the others may **follow**. (**clears his throat** as he is nervous) In the old days, the people of Japan believed the sun **goddess** and the god of night were sister and brother. The sun goddess made the **crops** grow and the trees bloom, so people loved her. But the god of night brought **evil spirits** to harm the land and the people **feared** him.

Carol: (starts sharing after Ben stops) Soon the god of night **grew jealous** of his sister. He wanted her to **go away** so he could keep the **earth** dark forever. One day the sun goddess was sitting in her **temple**. Her brother came behind her with a big sack.

George: (speaks slowly and **dramatically**) He opened the sack and a **huge snake** came out of the sack. The evil brother put the snake around the chair of the sun goddess. She **was so scared** that she went **to hide** into a cave and did not come out.

Monique: (continues the legend) So, the earth became dark. The god of night **destroyed** all the crops and **frightened** people. Children were scared to go out to play. So, some **representatives** of the people went to the cave and asked the sun goddess to come out. But she was so scared and did not come out.

Paolo: After that, people went to a **wise** man and asked for help. The wise man said: "Make noise. Maybe she will be **curious** and come out to see what is happening." Many people gathered at the cave. They **beat drums**, **rang bells**, and sang songs. The sun goddess heard the noise and became very curious. Finally, she came out.

Stephen: When people saw her, they surrounded her and the earth became bright again. Everybody was happy.

Ming: When the god of night saw the happy people, he **felt sorry** for what he had done. He **promised** never to do it again.

Mr. Knowitall: Now I understand why your teacher is so proud of you. You did a wonderful job sharing the Japenese lengend in class today and your English progress is **remarkable**. Also, your self confidence is strong and I am very proud of you. Thanks.

Practice Your Knowledge

Exercise #1—Vocabulary study

Task 1—Check the meaning of the following words in your dictionary. Copy the definitions.

Task 2—Find the sentence with the same word from the text and copy it or write your own sentence. Follow the example with the first word **"satisfied"**:

Definition—fulfill a need or a desire

Sentence—Mr. Knowitall is satisfied with his students' progress in academic English.

❏ progress
Definition . . . .
. . . .
Sentence . . . .
. . . .

❏ reflect
Definition . . . .
. . . .
Sentence . . . .
. . . .

❏ subject
Definition . . . .
. . . .
Sentence . . . .
. . . .

❏ to plan
Definition . . . .
. . . .
Sentence . . . .
. . . .

❏ step
Definition . . . .
. . . .
Sentence . . . .
. . . .

❏ to call
Definition . . . .
. . . .
Sentence . . . .
. . . .

❏ self-confidence
Definition . . . .
. . . .
Sentence . . . .
. . . .

❑ slow

Definition . . . .
. . . .

Sentence . . . .
. . . .

❑ usually

Definition . . . .
. . . .

Sentence . . . .
. . . .

❑ classmates

Definition . . . .
. . . .

Sentence . . . .
. . . .

❑ self-confident

Definition . . . .
. . . .

Sentence . . . .
. . . .

❑ intimidated

Definition . . . .
. . . .

Sentence . . . .
. . . .

❑ fluent

Definition . . . .
. . . .

Sentence . . . .
. . . .

❑ supportive

Definition . . . .
. . . .

Sentence . . . .
. . . .

137

❑ to master
Definition . . . .
. . . .
Sentence . . . .
. . . .
❑ teammates
Definition . . . .
. . . .
Sentence . . . .
. . . .
❑ explain
Definition . . . .
. . . .
Sentence . . . .
. . . .
❑ proud
Definition . . . .
. . . .
Sentence . . . .
. . . .
❑ follow
Definition . . . .
. . . .
Sentence . . . .
. . . .
❑ goddess
Definition . . . .
. . . .
Sentence . . . .
. . . .
❑ god
Definition . . . .
. . . .
Sentence . . . .
. . . .

❑ crop
Definition . . . .
. . . .
Sentence . . . .
. . . .
❑ evil
Definition . . . .
. . . .
Sentence . . . .
. . . .
❑ spirit
Definition . . . .
. . . .
Sentence . . . .
. . . .
❑ to fear
Definition . . . .
. . . .
Sentence . . . .
. . . .
❑ earth
Definition . . . .
. . . .
Sentence . . . .
. . . .
❑ temple
Definition . . . .
. . . .
Sentence . . . .
. . . .
❑ dramatically
Definition . . . .
. . . .
Sentence . . . .
. . . .

139

❑ huge
Definition . . . .
. . . .
Sentence . . . .
. . . .
❑ snake
Definition . . . .
. . . .
Sentence . . . .
. . . .
❑ hide
Definition . . . .
. . . .
Sentence . . . .
. . . .
❑ destroy
Definition . . . .
. . . .
Sentence . . . .
. . . .
❑ frightened
Definition . . . .
. . . .
Sentence . . . .
. . . .
❑ representative
Definition . . . .
. . . .
Sentence . . . .
. . . .
❑ wise
Definition . . . .
. . . .
Sentence . . . .
. . . .

❑ curious

Definition . . . .
. . . .
Sentence . . . .
. . . .

❑ promise

Definition . . . .
. . . .
Sentence . . . .
. . . .

❑ remarkable

Definition . . . .
. . . .
Sentence . . . .
. . . .

Exercise #2—Check if you understood the story. Use the information from the story "When the Sun Went Away" to answer the questions:

1. What did people of Japan believe in old days? _____
    _____

2. What did the brother (god of night) do to his sister? _____
    _____

3. Who gathered at the cave? _____
    _____

4. What did they do there? _____
    _____

5. What happened when the sun goddess came out of the cave? _____
    _____

6. Number the events below in the order they happened (1,2,3 . . .).
    _____ The god of night put a snake around his sister's chair._____
    People gathered in front of the cave and made noise._____ The sun
    goddess ran into the cave and would not come out. _____ The
    sun goddess became curious and came out of the cave.

7. What is the main idea of the last paragraph of the story? Circle one of the following:
   1. The sun goddess came out of the cave.
   2. The god of night promised not to trick his sister again.
   3. The people were happy that sun goddess came out of the cave.

Exercise #3 : VOCABULARY BUILDING—Insert the right word from the list in the blanks in the following sentences. Sentences are taken from the story "When the Sun Went Away".

subject	self-confidence	frightened	supportive
classmates	fluent	intimidated	earth
representatives	wise	remarkable	satisfied

- Mr.Knowitall is _____ with his students' progress in English but he would like to see that progress reflected in the _____ students are studying at school, like Social Studies or English Language Arts.
- Show a little _____.
- Usually I am self confident but when I am in classes with my Canadian _____, I am _____ because I feel I am not _____ in English.
- It makes me very uncomfortable but my classmates are very _____.
- He wanted her to go away so he could keep the _____ dark forever.
- The god of night destroyed all the crops and _____ people.
- So, some _____ of the people went to the cave and asked the sun goddess to come out.
- After that, people went to a_____ man and asked for help.
- You did a wonderful job sharing the Japenese lengend in class today and your English progress is _____.

Exercise #4: VOCABULARY BUILDING—Use the words you learned in the story "When the Sun Went Away" in a new context. Make the necessary changes.

classmates	fluent	intimidated	earth
representatives	wise	remarkable	satisfied
subject	self-confidence	frightened	supportive

- The child was _____ by the darkness and started to cry.
- My mother is never _____ with my progress in school.
- His _____ gave him a very warm welcome.
- I do all my homework every day and that has helped me become _____ in English.
- Persons elected to lead us are the _____ of the people.
- My favorite _____ at school is Math.
- Learning more academic words builds my _____ in class.
- I enjoy learning important information in the field of _____ science.
- After the dangerous accident, she has made a _____ improvement.
- Children are _____ by strangers.
- There was a snake in the garden and my little brother was very _____.
- It is _____ to plan your study time well.

Exercise #5—Find the secret word and write a sentence with it.

- atitevenserper _____ . . . .
  . . . .
  . . . .
- elbakramer _____ . . . .
  . . . .
  . . . .

- tedidatimin _____ . . . .
. . . .
. . . .
- iveportpus _____ . . . .
. . . .
. . . .
- edtenighrf _____ . . . .
. . . .
. . . .
- woolfl _____ . . . .
. . . .
. . . .

Grammar Point—Past Tense of Verbs-In English, verbs have different tenses. Let us learn how to correctly use past tense. **Past Tense** is used when:

- we talk about an action that was repeated in the past, e. x.: When she **was** a little girl, Mary **played** with dolls.
- we tell a story from the past, e.x.: In the old days, people of Japan **believed** that there **was** a sun goddess and a god of night.
- we speak about a number of actions we did in the past, e. x.: Yesterday, I **went** to school and then I **helped** my friend to do the homework. (we use these words in sentences with verbs in the past tense—yesterday, last night, after that, last year, a month ago, when I was a little boy)

ATTENTION! Verbs change their form in the Past Tense. Usually they take an "ed" at the end. These are called Regular Verbs, e. x: I **work** today. I **worked** yesterday. Sometimes, some verbs change their form completely in the Past Tense. These are called Irregular Verbs, e. x: I **speak** today. I **spoke** yesterday. Some verbs do not change at all in the past tense, e. x.: Today I **put** my book in the bag. Yesterday I **put** my book in the bag.

Exercise #6—Writers make frequent mistakes with irregular verbs. They add an incorrect *ed* to the end of an irregular verb. Find the mistakes and write the correct sentence.

- Olivia **feeled** like exercising yesterday, so she **putted** on her bathing suit and **drived** to the YMCA. . . . .
. . . .
. . . .
. . . .

- She **swimed** so far and got so hungry that only a large pepperoni pizza would satisfy her hunger . . . .
. . . .
. . . .
. . . .

- After that, Olivia <u>**drived**</u> to her friend's house to finish the homework but she **forgeted** to bring her textbook with her. . . . .
. . . .
. . . .
. . . .

Homework—Check the verbs in the lesson "When the Sun Went Away" and put them in the correct column—Present or Past Tense

Present Tense	Past Tense

Supplemental Reading—Choose the best tittle for the following short story: a) The Happy Kitten; b) Dinah and the Kitten; c) Mrs. Brown Cat; d) Cat's New Name;

Dinah was sitting at the table but she was not eating her food. "What are you thinking about?", asked her mother. "Can I help, Dinah?". Dinah looked up. "Oh, I have to find a home for the kitten I found yesterday." Almost everyone I know already has a cat or a dog. Dinah's mother said,

"Have you thought about Mrs. Brown? She doesn't have any pets, does she?" "Thank you, Mom, that's a great idea. Why didn't I think of that before? Mrs. Brown likes animals. She had a cat once, but it died. I think she will really like this kitten!"

Dinah began to eat. When her food was finished, she went over to the kitten. The little kitten was drinking milk from a bowl on the kitchen floor. "Come on," said Dinah as she picked it up. "I'm taking you to a new home." Mrs. Brown was delighted with the kitten. "I have wanted a new cat ever since old Mr. Whiskers died. Now I have one. Thanks so much for thinking of me, Dinah. Have you already given it a name?" Dinah shook her head, "No, the kitten has no name." Mrs. Brown replied, "Then that is what I shall call it. The kitten's name will be No Name." Both Dinah and Mrs. Brown laughed as No Name purred. It seemed to be purring, "I like my new name, **No Name**."

Study   **STUDY TIP**—We need to develop a concentration-span —the time between starting a task to the time we find our minds wandering. This is because our brain deals with information in a very special way. Learn to increase your concentration span by making learning enjoyable.

SPOT THE MISTAKE—Find the mistakes and fix them. Write the correct sentence:

This snake is trying to destroy the crops and frighten the people. . . . .
. . . .
. . . .
. . . .
. . . .
. . . .

REMEMBER THIS—You can always consult a dictionary when you have a question about the correct form of an irregular verb. See the chart at the end of this book, too.

DID YOU KNOW?—A giraffe can clean its ears with its 21-inch tongue.

DID YOU KNOW?—Canadians consume more macaroni and cheese than any other nation in the world.

<u>LANGUAGE</u> <u>BANK</u>—In this lesson you learned:

Active words	**Recycled words**	**Passive words**
1. goddess	1. elegant	1. action
2. god	2. gentleman	2. repeated
3. satisfied	3. feeling	3. doll
4. progress	4. nervous	4. attention
5. crop	5. proficiency	5. completely
6. reflect	6. appreciate	6. look up
7. evil	7. share	7. almost
8. spirit	8. answer	8. kitten
9. to fear	9. culture	9. bowl
10. jealous	10. uncomfortable	10. pick up
11. subject	11. honour	11. delighted
12. to plan	12. exactly	12. reply
13. step	13. legend	13. purred
14. call	14. believe	14. concentration
15. temple	15. harm	15. span
16. self-confidence	16. dark	16. wandering
17. slow	17. cave	17. brain
18. huge	18. surrounded	18. increase
19. snake	19. bright	19. giraffe
20. usually	20. special	20. tongue
21. classmate	21. way	
22. destroy	22. enjoy(able)	
23. frighten		
24. self-confident		
25. intimidated		
26. fluent		
27. curious	**Expressions:** do(ing) fine, nothing to worry	
28. beat	about, speak highly of (somebody), clear the	
29. drum	throat, grow jealous, go away, to be scared, beat	
30. ring (rang)	a drum, ring a bell, feel sorry	

31. bell
32. supportive
33. to master
34. teammates
35. explain
36. proud
37. follow
38. earth
39. dramatically
40. hide
41. representative
42. wise
43. promise
44. remarkable

Lesson #8—Thanksgiving

Learning Goals: A—Understand the story
B—Learn new words
C—Learn how to use This & That

Language Structure Point: THIS & THAT

(It is the beginning of October and **Thanksgiving celebration** is **around the corner**. Mr.Knowitall plans **to roast** two **turkeys** for his students for the Thanksgiving dinner. Today he plans to talk about this celebration and **characteristics** of food preparation in different cultures.)

Mr. Knowitall: Good morning, Folks. It has been raining all week and I have been reflecting about the remarkable self-confidence the **settlers** must have shown in **surviving** their first winter in this new country. They did not know much about the **climate**, the earth and the crops that could grow in this new land. I am **amazed** at their **survival skills**.

Carol: (reflecting) The first steps in this new country were not easy for us, also. We called our family back home and tried to explain the difficulties to master the language and the new lifestyle. However, our experience was **nothing compared** to the first settlers.

George: Our experience was not **easy either** but, **at least**, we did not need to be on a ship for months and then **ride** a **horse** or pull a cart over the snow covered **mountains** and **muddy valleys**. We **flew** to this country and that is a much more enjoyable trip.

Monique: The first experiences in a new country are very interesting. I **arrived** here last year **on the eve** of Thanksgiving and I could not understand the meaning of this celebration. Who do we thank and why? Can you explain that to us Mr. Knowitall, please?

Mr. Knowitall: (smiling) I would be happy to do that, Monique but first let us see if anybody knows anything about the story **behind** Thanksgiving. (turns to the class) Does anybody want to share anything?

Paolo: (satisfied at his knowledge of technology) I don't know anything but I can **check** that information in the Internet.

Stephen: Yes, but my dear Paolo that, would **mean** that the computer is sharing not you. Mr. Knowitall asked if (**stresses** the word) ANYBODY, not anything, wants to share a story. (everybody laughs at Stephen's joke)

Ming: I have read that Canadian Thanksgiving is celebrated on the second Monday in October. On Thanksgiving Day Canadians give thanks for a successful **harvest**. The harvest season falls earlier in Canada compared to the United States **due to** the **simple** fact that Canada is further north and that is why Canadians celebrate Thanksgiving in October and Americans in November.

Mr. Knowitall: Yes, you are correct, Ming. The history of Thanksgiving in Canada goes back to an English **explorer**, Martin Frobisher, who had been trying to find a northern **passage** to the **Orient.** In the year 1578, he held a **formal ceremony**, in what is now called Newfoundland, to give thanks for **surviving** the long **journey**. This is considered the first Canadian Thanksgiving. At the same time, French settlers, having **crossed** the **ocean** and arrived in Canada with explorer Samuel de Champlain, also held **huge feasts** of thanks.

Carol: I think all kinds of celebrations **include** some kind of baked foods. However, I **am confused** because sometimes I **encounter** the word "bake" and sometimes the word "roast" with almost the same meaning. Are they the same, Mr. Knowitall?

Mr. Knowitall: Both words can be used **interchangibly**. However, some **chefs distinguish** between the two words based on temperature, with roasting **implying** greater **heat** and thus faster and more browning of the food than baking. Others may **prefer** to use the word "roasting" **specifically** for meats, **poultry** and vegetables, but use the term "baking" for bread, cakes, pies, cookies, fish and other seafood. The **dry** heat of baking changes the form of **starches** in the food and causes its outer **surfaces** to brown, giving it an **attractive** look and **crispy crust**.

George: I can tell when I pass by our neighborhood bakery because it is a place that smells very nicely. On the window there are cakes of all shapes and sizes. I can get a little piece of cake for two dollars.

Monique: For two dollars, I can get that slice of cheesecake. I like that bakery. That is Mrs. Sweet, the **owner** of this bakery.

Paolo: For Mother's day we **ordered** a fruit cake from this bakery. My sister and I went to the bakery to pick that cake up that afternoon.

Carol: It is so attractive to see all kinds of baked good in Mrs. Sweet's bakery. On the top shelf of this bakery stands that big white **wedding** cake. That is not our cake, it is too **fancy**. This one, this chocolate cake is our cake.

Stephen: I believe that baking is a very ancient way of cooking. In ancient history, the first **evidence** of baking happened when humans took grass **grains**, soaked them in water, and mixed everything together, making it into a kind of **paste**. The paste was cooked by putting it onto a hot rock, making the first bread-like food.

Ming: Chinese do not bake a lot at home. Most Chinese **households** do not have **ovens** because they don't need ovens. Chinese food is usually prepared by stir-frying, boiling, or **steaming** the food on stove-top cookers of different kinds. Baking and roasting are not used by home cooks but by bakers.

George: I love the crispy surface of baked food.

Mr. Knowitall: As it is your first time that you will celebrate Thanksgiving in this new country and I am thankful to have you in my class, Mrs. Knowitall and I want to invite all of you to join us for Thanksgiving dinner next week. We will have a traditional Thanksgiving dinner with a roasted turkey and delicious **stuffing**, sweet patatoes, cranberry sauce, and a nicely baked pumpkin pie.

All the students: (very happy) Thank you Mr. Knowitall.

Practice Your Knowledge

Exercise #1—Vocabulary study

Task 1—Check the meaning of the following words in your dictionary. Copy the definitions.

Task 2—Find the sentence with the same word from the text and copy it or write your own sentence. Follow the example with the first word **"roast"**:

Definition—cook meat or vegetables by dry heat, usually in an oven
Sentence—I like the crispy surface of roasted turkey.

❑ Thanksgiving
Definition . . . .
. . . .
Sentence . . . .
. . . .
❑ celebration
Definition . . . .
. . . .
Sentence . . . .
. . . .

❏ turkey

Definition . . . .
. . . .

Sentence . . . .
. . . .

❏ climate

Definition . . . .
. . . .

Sentence . . . .
. . . .

❏ characteristic

Definition . . . .
. . . .

Sentence . . . .
. . . .

❏ settlers

Definition . . . .
. . . .

Sentence . . . .
. . . .

❏ survive

Definition . . . .
. . . .

Sentence . . . .
. . . .

❏ amazed

Definition . . . .
. . . .

Sentence . . . .
. . . .

❏ skill

Definition . . . .
. . . .

Sentence . . . .
. . . .

❑ nothing

Definition . . . .

. . . .

Sentence . . . .

. . . .

❑ compare

Definition . . . .

. . . .

Sentence . . . .

. . . .

❑ easy

Definition . . . .

. . . .

Sentence . . . .

. . . .

❑ either

Definition . . . .

. . . .

Sentence . . . .

. . . .

❑ mountain

Definition . . . .

. . . .

Sentence . . . .

. . . .

❑ valley

Definition . . . .

. . . .

Sentence . . . .

. . . .

❑ muddy

Definition . . . .

. . . .

Sentence . . . .

. . . .

❑ arrive

Definition . . . .

. . . .

Sentence . . . .

. . . .

❑ behind

Definition . . . .

. . . .

Sentence . . . .

. . . .

❑ check

Definition . . . .

. . . .

Sentence . . . .

. . . .

❑ mean (v)

Definition . . . .

. . . .

Sentence . . . .

. . . .

❑ stress (v)

Definition . . . .

. . . .

Sentence . . . .

. . . .

❑ harvest

Definition . . . .

. . . .

Sentence . . . .

. . . .

❑ simple

Definition . . . .

. . . .

Sentence . . . .

. . . .

❑ October
Definition . . . .
. . . .
Sentence . . . .
. . . .

❑ November
Definition . . . .
. . . .
Sentence . . . .
. . . .

❑ explorer
Definition . . . .
. . . .
Sentence . . . .
. . . .

❑ passage
Definition . . . .
. . . .
Sentence . . . .
. . . .

❑ Orient
Definition . . . .
. . . .
Sentence . . . .
. . . .

❑ **cross (v)**
Definition . . . .
. . . .
Sentence . . . .
. . . .

❑ formal
Definition . . . .
. . . .
Sentence . . . .
. . . .

❏ ceremony
Definition . . . .
. . . .
Sentence . . . .
. . . .
❏ journey
Definition . . . .
. . . .
Sentence . . . .
. . . .
❏ ocean
Definition . . . .
. . . .
Sentence . . . .
. . . .
❏ huge
Definition . . . .
. . . .
Sentence . . . .
. . . .
❏ feast
Definition . . . .
. . . .
Sentence . . . .
. . . .
❏ include
Definition . . . .
. . . .
Sentence . . . .
. . . .
❏ encounter
Definition . . . .
. . . .
Sentence . . . .
. . . .

❏ interchangeably
Definition . . . .
. . . .
Sentence . . . .
. . . .
❏ chef
Definition . . . .
. . . .
Sentence . . . .
. . . .
❏ distinguish
Definition . . . .
. . . .
Sentence . . . .
. . . .
❏ imply
Definition . . . .
. . . .
Sentence . . . .
. . . .
❏ heat
Definition . . . .
. . . .
Sentence . . . .
. . . .
❏ prefer
Definition . . . .
. . . .
Sentence . . . .
. . . .
❏ specifically
Definition . . . .
. . . .
Sentence . . . .
. . . .

❑ poultry

Definition . . . .
. . . .

Sentence . . . .
. . . .

❑ dry

Definition . . . .
. . . .

Sentence . . . .
. . . .

❑ starch

Definition . . . .
. . . .

Sentence . . . .
. . . .

❑ surface

Definition . . . .
. . . .

Sentence . . . .
. . . .

❑ attractive

Definition . . . .
. . . .

Sentence . . . .
. . . .

❑ crispy

Definition . . . .
. . . .

Sentence . . . .
. . . .

❑ crust

Definition . . . .
. . . .

Sentence . . . .
. . . .

❑ owner
Definition . . . .
. . . .
Sentence . . . .
. . . .
❑ order (v)
Definition . . . .
. . . .
Sentence . . . .
. . . .
❑ fancy
Definition . . . .
. . . .
Sentence . . . .
. . . .
❑ evidence
Definition . . . .
. . . .
Sentence . . . .
. . . .
❑ wedding
Definition . . . .
. . . .
Sentence . . . .
. . . .
❑ cranberry
Definition . . . .
. . . .
Sentence . . . .
. . . .
❑ pumpkin
Definition . . . .
. . . .
Sentence . . . .
. . . .

❏ grain
Definition . . . .
. . . .
Sentence . . . .
. . . .
❏ paste
Definition . . . .
. . . .
Sentence . . . .
. . . .
❏ household
Definition . . . .
. . . .
Sentence . . . .
. . . .
❏ oven
Definition . . . .
. . . .
Sentence . . . .
. . . .
❏ steam
Definition . . . .
. . . .
Sentence . . . .
. . . .
❏ stuffing
Definition . . . .
. . . .
Sentence . . . .
. . . .

Exercise #2—Check for understanding. Read the story and answer the questions:

1. What is Thanksgiving celebration? _____
_____

2. When is it celebrated in Canada and when in America? Why? _____

3. Where did my sister and I go? _____

4. Why did we go the Mr. Sweet's bakery? _____

5. Are all the cakes the same? Describe _____

6. What can you buy for two dollars in the bakery? _____

7. Is a wedding cake attractive? Describe it. _____

8. What foods are usually served for Thanksgiving dinner?_____

Exercise #3—Find the secret word and write a sentence with it.

- yreranbcra_____ . . . .
  . . . .
  . . . .

- nahcgaeylbreint _____ . . . .
  . . . .

- iuhsstingid_____ . . . .
  . . . .

- rreolpxe_____ . . . .
  . . . .

- uocnterne_____ . . . .
  . . . .

- ateimcl_____ . . . .
  . . . .
  . . . .

: VOCABULARY BUILDING—Insert the right word from the list in the blanks in the following sentences. Sentences are taken from the story "Thanksgiving".

celebration	formal	November	include
valleys	distinguish	implying	starch
household	harvest	surviving	settlers

- It has been raining all week and I have been reflecting about the remarkable self-confidence the _____ must have shown in surviving their first winter in this new country.
- It is the beginning of October and Thanksgiving _____ is around the corner.
- Our experience was not easy either but, at least, we did not need to be on a ship for months and then ride a horse or pull a cart over the snow covered mountains and muddy _____.
- On Thanksgiving Day Canadians give thanks for a successful _____.
- The harvest season falls earlier in Canada compared to the United States due to the simple fact that Canada is further north and that is why Canadians celebrate Thanksgiving in October and Americans in _____.
- In the year 1578, he held a _____ ceremony, in what is now called Newfoundland, to give thanks for _____ the long journey.
- However, some chefs _____ between the two words based on temperature, with roasting _____ greater heat and thus faster and more browning of the food than baking.
- The dry heat of baking changes the form of _____ in the food and causes its outer surfaces to brown, giving it an attractive look and crispy crust.
- Most Chinese _____ do not have ovens because they don't need ovens. Chinese food is usually prepared by stir-frying, boiling, or steaming the food on stove-top cookers of different kinds.
- I think all kinds of celebrations _____ some kind of baked foods.

Exercise #5: VOCABULARY BUILDING—Use the words you learned in the story "Thanksgiving" in a new context. Make the necessary changes.

valleys	distinguish	implying	starch
celebration	formal	November	include
household	harvest	surviving	settlers

* The tax for this coat is not_____ in the price.
* _____ is the eleventh month of the year.
* We are preparing a huge _____ for our mother's birthday.
* In order to graduate from high school, we need to master _____ English.
* She has _____ herself as the best basketball player in the team.
* The _____ to the New World must have had huge _____ skills.
* I love to run down the _____ in spring and pick beautiful flowers.
* There are four people in our _____.
* _____ time is a very busy time in my grandfather's farm.
* My doctor advised me to start a no _____ diet due to my high blood pressure.
* Is he _____ that I cheated in the last test?

Grammar Point—**This** and **That** are used to show where things or people are situated.

This —points to the things that are near the speaker.

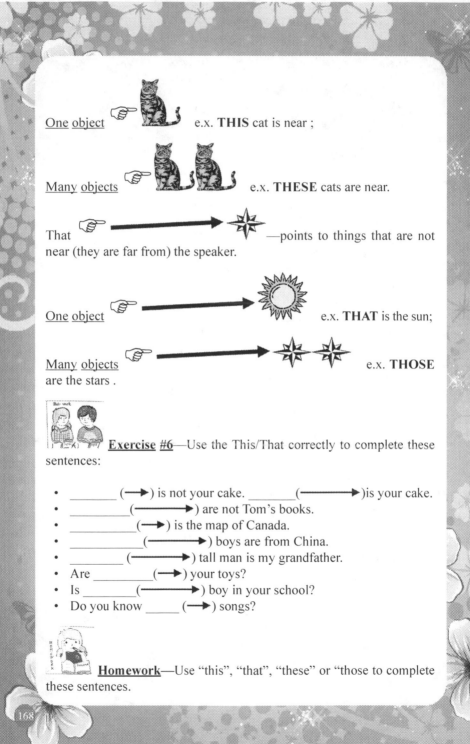

One object　e.x. **THIS** cat is near ;

Many objects　e.x. **THESE** cats are near.

That　—points to things that are not near (they are far from) the speaker.

One object　e.x. **THAT** is the sun;

Many objects　e.x. **THOSE** are the stars .

Exercise #6—Use the This/That correctly to complete these sentences:

- _____ (——►) is not your cake. _____(————►)is your cake.
- _____(————►) are not Tom's books.
- _____(——►) is the map of Canada.
- _____(————►) boys are from China.
- _____(————►) tall man is my grandfather.
- Are _____(——►) your toys?
- Is _____(————►) boy in your school?
- Do you know _____ (——►) songs?

Homework—Use "this", "that", "these" or "those to complete these sentences.

1. I need to stop for a coffee. Is _____ all right with you?
2. Do you like _____ trousers? I bought them yesterday.
3. Look at _____ man over there! He is my new teacher.
4. Her new house cost over half a million dollars. _____ a lot of money.
5. _____ boots that she is wearing look very expensive to me.
6. My grandmother never wore trousers when she was young. In _____ days it wasn't acceptable.
7. I'm going to Calgary again _____ week-end. Do you want to come?
8. Yes, let's go to the restaurant tonight. _____ is a great idea.
9. Oh, I love _____ pair of trousers. I'm going to buy myself a pair?
10. Here we are. _____ is where I live.

Supplemental Reading—Choose the best tittle for the following short story: a) Walt Sells Seeds; b) Father's Advice; c) The Big Businessman; d) Buying a New Toy.

Walt was selling flower seeds. He was going from house to house in his neighborhood. For every pack of seeds he sold he got to keep a nickel. Walt had big dreams about the money he was going to make. "If I sell 100 packs of seed, I'll make $5," he told Paolo. "If I sell 1000 packs, I will make $50. I can make even more than that if I try." By the end of the afternoon Walt was tired. He shook his head sadly. He hadn't made anywhere near what he thought he would. All he had sold were fourteen packs of seed. He was going home. Walter's dad watched him come slowly up the sidewalk. "Well, how did the big business do?" Walt shrugged his shoulders. "I guess I struck out. I only made 80 cents. That's nowhere near $5, much less $50."

Walt's dad patted him on the shoulders. "Selling is hard work," he said, "but look at it this way: You have 80 cents now that you did not have early this afternoon." Walter's face broke into a smile. "You are right, Dad. Those 80 cents are enough to buy that plastic model I've wanted."

All of a sudden Walt was no longer tired. He was even whistling as he went off to the toy store.

SPOT THE MISTAKE—Find the mistakes and fix them. Write the correct sentence:

This new settler has survived a trip through muddy valleys. . . . .
. . . .
. . . .
. . . .
. . . .
. . . .
. . . .
. . . .

REMEMBER THIS—We can put adverbs in different positions in sentences. There are three main positions but also a lot of exceptions. In English we **never** put an **adverb** between the **verb** and the **object**—We **often play handball**. CORRECT; We play often handball. WRONG

DID YOU KNOW?—Camels have three eyelids to protect themselves from blowing sand.

LANGUAGE BANK—In this lesson you learned:

Active words	Recycled words	Passive words
1. Thanksgiving	1. plan(v)	1. tax
2. celebration	2. dinner	2. coat
3. roast	3. culture	3. price
4. turkey	4. reflect	4. busy
5. climate	5. self-confidence	5. blood
6. bakery (ies)	6. remarkable	6. pressure
7. owner	7. crops	7. cheat
8. order	8. earth	8. fix
9. characteristic	9. food	9. necessary
10. settler	10. master(v)	10. weekend
11. wedding	11. explain	11. boots
12. survive	12. call	12. expensive
13. fancy	13 lifestyle	13. acceptable
14. survival	14. experience	
15. amazed	15. however	
16. skill	16. enjoyable	
17. nothing	17. pull a cart	
18. compare	18. interesting	
19. easy	19. anybody	
20. either	20. anything	
21. mountain	21. share	
22. valley	22. information	
23. muddy	23. satisfied	
24. arrive	24. celebrate	
25. behind	25. invite	
26. check	26. consider	
27. mean (v)	27. cheesecake	
28. stress (v)	28. neighbourhood	
29. harvest	29. ancient	
30. simple	30. usually	

31. October
32. November
33. explorer
34. passage
35. formal
36. ceremony
37. journey
38. cross(v)
39. feast
40. ocean
41. huge
42. include
43. encounter
44. interchangeably
45. chef
46. distinguish
47. imply
48. heat
49. prefer
50. dry
51. specifically
52. poultry
53. starch
54. surface
55. attractive
56. crispy
57. crust
58. cranberry
59. evidence
60. pumpkin
61. grain
62. paste
63. household
64. oven
65. steam
66. stuffing

Expressions: (to be) is around the corner, on the eve of, due to, to be confused, ride a horse

THEME #2

Special People
Special Deeds

Lesson #1—The Town Hero

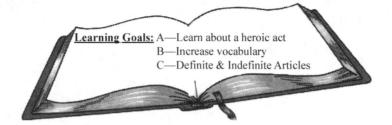

Learning Goals: A—Learn about a heroic act
B—Increase vocabulary
C—Definite & Indefinite Articles

Language Focus: Articles

Context Clues—Pre-Reading: Check your vocabulary knowledge. Fill in the circle before the word with the same meaning as the bold word in the sentence.

❖ Schools are trying to ensure that no student **gets hurt** in the basketball court. They have enforced strong rules for the use of the court. **"gets hurt"** means:

O become injured
O take care
O receive a pass
O help somebody get across the street.

❖ The bus arrived late in the station. There were a number of **commuters** waiting at the station to go to school and work. **"commuters"** means:

O people who cook for others
O community members
O regular travelers from home to school or work
O people who deliver newspapers

❖ The bus tickets are getting more expensive each day. However, many commuters have no other way to go to work or school. Therefore, they continue to **ride** the bus or the train. **"ride"** means:

○ learn how to drive the bus or train
○ travel as passengers in a bus or train
○ buy a new car or bus
○ clean a vehicle that is dirty

❖ A grade eleven student suffered from a heart disease and was put on strong medication. Yesterday she was taken to hospital because she **fainted** in her gym class. **"fainted"** means:

○ participate in a practice session
○ lose (lost) consciousness briefly
○ score a goal in the gym class
○ be absent from school due to illness

❖ The new driver was very nervous. He was taking the behind the **steering wheel** test. **"steering wheel"** means:

○ the wheel of a heavy truck
○ the wheel of fortune game show
○ a means of guiding a vehicle
○ your uncle's wife driving test

❖ There was a snow storm last night and many drivers lost control of their vehicles. My friend was driving in an icy road and he **swerved** the car into a ditch to avoid hitting a tree. **"swerve"** means:

○ turn away from direct course
○ learn how to drive in icy roads
○ turn to the right and to the left
○ run away from dangerous roads

❖ My grandmother still drives at 80 years of age. However, it is hard for her because she is so short that she can hardly reach the **brake pedal** now. **"brake pedal"** means:

O break off a relationship with her next door neighbor
O a foot operated part of a vehicle that is used to slow down or stop
   a vehicle
O make something move faster than ever before the accident
O play a musical instrument that was found in a museum in
   Toronto

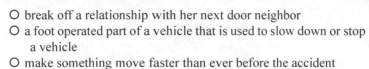 Before you read the story, look at this picture
and answer these questions:

What does this picture tell you about the story you are about to read? _____
_____
_____

Have you ever been in a car accident? _____
_____

What did you do when you understood what was happening? _____
_____

What are the main reasons people get involved in a car accident? _____
_____

Have you heard of people who help others in a case of car accident? What
did they do to help? _____
_____

What should we do in case of an emergency? _____
_____
_____

Read the story "The town hero" and answer the questions that follow

The Town Hero

[2]This story happened in a small town in Alberta. Up to 15 **centimetres** of **snow**, **combined** with a train derailment that **blocked** the **railway tracks** used by the city train (West Coast) **service**, had led to long **delays** for the **commuters**. The climate changed dramatically and made the bus **trip** to school very difficult that day. The **weather forecast announced** that the weather would not be improving anytime soon. Another major **headache**, the snow, had also delayed school buses **throughout** the School District. The winter weather, which was at its most **extreme** that day, had hit the **region** since last weekend. This might have **contributed** to a number of car **crashes** like the one that killed a 20-year-old woman on Sunday.

On a day like that, a young student, Albi, became a **hero** at his school and became the talk of the city. The tenth—grade student brought a **run-away bus** to a **safe stop**. He **saved** thirty of his classmates from **getting hurt**. Such an action made him **popular**. This is what happened: Albi was riding to school on the school bus as usual that morning. The bus **driver fainted** at the **wheel.** The bus began to **swerve**. It started going **faster** and faster on the **streets** of the snow-covered and **icy** town.

Albi **rushed** to the driver's side and **instantly** understood that the driver could not control the bus due to a health condition. Albi's life and the lives of his friends were in real danger. Albi made a quick decision. He **pushed** the **brake pedal** to **slow down** the bus. Then he **turned** the **steering wheel** and brought the run—away bus to a safe stop in the school **driveway**.

What had happened to the driver? The driver had been sick for a number of days. He had to take some strong **medicine** that morning. To **make matters worse**, the roads were **frozen** and it was snowing heavily. After the accident, the doctor who **examined** the driver **concluded** that the

2   The idea for this story was adapted from the real story, "After Driver Passes Out, Boy, 12, Halts School Bus"—published by New York Times, December 21, 1991

medicine had caused him to faint. An accident like that could have been very dangerous for all the students in the bus. Albi's heroic **act** saved the lives of so many of his friends. He became very **popular** in his school and was distinguished as the town hero.

Practice Your Knowledge

Exercise #1—Vocabulary study

Task 1—Check the meaning of the following words in your dictionary. Copy the definitions.

Task 2—Find the sentence with the same word from the text and copy it or write your own sentence. Follow the example with the word **"happen"**:

"**happen**" Definition—to take place,
        Sentence—This story <u>happened</u> last summer in my town.

➢ derailment
Definition . . . .
. . . .
Sentence . . . .
. . . .
➢ tracks
Definition . . . .
. . . .
Sentence . . . .
. . . .
➢ commuter
Definition . . . .
. . . .
Sentence . . . .
. . . .

➢ weather forecast
Definition . . . .
. . . .
Sentence . . . .
. . . .
➢ major
Definition . . . .
. . . .
Sentence . . . .
. . . .
➢ brought to a stop
Definition . . . .
. . . .
Sentence . . . .
. . . .
➢ run away bus
Definition . . . .
. . . .
Sentence . . . .
. . . .
➢ safe
Definition . . . .
. . . .
Sentence . . . .
. . . .
➢ delay
Definition . . . .
. . . .
Sentence . . . .
. . . .
➢ getting hurt
Definition . . . .
. . . .
Sentence . . . .
. . . .

➢ faint
Definition . . . .
. . . .
Sentence . . . .
. . . .

➢ steering wheel
Definition . . . .
. . . .
Sentence . . . .
. . . .

➢ swerve
Definition . . . .
. . . .
Sentence . . . .
. . . .

➢ fast
Definition . . . .
. . . .
Sentence . . . .

➢ rush
Definition . . . .
. . . .
Sentence . . . .
. . . .

➢ brake pedal
Definition . . . .
. . . .
Sentence . . . .
. . . .

➢ slow down
Definition . . . .
. . . .
Sentence . . . .
. . . .

➤ medicine

Definition . . . .
. . . .

Sentence . . . .
. . . .

➤ accident

Definition . . . .
. . . .

Sentence . . . .
. . . .

➤ driveway

Definition . . . .
. . . .

Sentence . . . .
. . . .

➤ deed

Definition . . . .
. . . .

Sentence . . . .
. . . .

➤ centimeter

Definition . . . .
. . . .

Sentence . . . .
. . . .

➤ combine (with . . . .)

Definition . . . .
. . . .

Sentence . . . .
. . . .

➤ block

Definition . . . .
. . . .

Sentence . . . .
. . . .

➢ railway
Definition . . . .
. . . .
Sentence . . . .
. . . .

➢ service
Definition . . . .
. . . .
Sentence . . . .
. . . .

➢ announce
Definition . . . .
. . . .
Sentence . . . .
. . . .

➢ weather
Definition . . . .
. . . .
Sentence . . . .
. . . .

➢ headache
Definition . . . .
. . . .
Sentence . . . .
. . . .

➢ throughout
Definition . . . .
. . . .
Sentence . . . .
. . . .

➢ extreme
Definition . . . .
. . . .
Sentence . . . .
. . . .

➤ region
Definition . . . .
. . . .
Sentence . . . .
. . . .
➤ contribute (to . . . .)
Definition . . . .
. . . .
Sentence . . . .
. . . .
➤ crash
Definition . . . .
. . . .
Sentence . . . .
. . . .
➤ hero
Definition . . . .
. . . .
Sentence . . . .
. . . .
➤ driver
Definition . . . .
. . . .
Sentence . . . .
. . . .
➤ wheel
Definition . . . .
. . . .
Sentence . . . .
. . . .
➤ rush
Definition . . . .
. . . .
Sentence . . . .
. . . .

➢ street

Definition . . . .
. . . .

Sentence . . . .
. . . .

➢ frozen

Definition . . . .
. . . .

Sentence . . . .
. . . .

➢ icy

Definition . . . .
. . . .

Sentence . . . .
. . . .

➢ examine

Definition . . . .
. . . .

Sentence . . . .
. . . .

➢ conclude

Definition . . . .
. . . .

Sentence . . . .
. . . .

➢ act

Definition . . . .
. . . .

Sentence . . . .
. . . .

➢ instantly

Definition . . . .
. . . .

Sentence . . . .
. . . .

➢ turn

Definition . . . .
. . . .
Sentence . . . .
. . . .

Exercise #2: VOCABULARY BUILDING—Insert the right word in the blanks. Use the words from the list below. The sentences are taken from the story "The Town Hero".

run-away bus	derailment	commuters	delays
the weather forecast	fainted	brake pedal	slow down
swerve	steering wheel	town hero	

1. The trip to school was not expected to be easy, as _____ _____ announced, the weather would not be improving anytime soon.
2. The tenth-grade student brought a _____ _____ to a safe stop.
3. Up to 15 centimetres of snow, combined with a train _____ that blocked the tracks used by the West Coast Express, had led to long _____ for the _____.
4. The bus driver _____ at the wheel.
5. He pushed the _____ _____ to _____ _____ the bus.
6. The bus began to _____.
7. Then he turned the _____ _____ and brought the _____ to a safe stop in the school driveway.
8. He became a _____ _____.

Exercise #3: VOCABULARY BUILDING—Use the words you learned in the story "The Town Hero" in a new context:

derailment	commuters	medical	delays
the weather forecast	fainted	brake pedal	slow down
swerve	steering wheel	run away bus	popular

1. According to police, the accident happened due to a _____ problem.
2. The snowstorm caused _____ during the morning commute.
3. The mudslides caused dangerous _____ of the train tracks.
4. In order to avoid hitting the little dog, the driver _____ the car into a ditch.
5. The tennis player checked the _____ _____ for the day of his next game.
6. The sick marathon runner _____ in the middle of the race.
7. The early morning _____ were braving the extreme weather conditions.
8. The boy who jumped into the river to save the little puppy has become _____ in his town.
9. Police officers put a spike belt on the street to _____ _____ the _____ _____ car.
10. The young man covered the _____ _____ of his brand new car with a smooth cotton cloth.

Exercise #4: VOCABULARY BUILDING—Match the words below with the definitions in the box.

1. . . . . **derailment**   a) well-liked, admired, accepted
2. . . . . **commuters**   b) a vehicle that ran off without control
3. . . . . **medical**   c) part of a vehicle that controls the movement
4. . . . . **delays**   d) turn sharply, change direction
5. . . . . **the weather forecast**   e) reduce speed by using the brakes
6. . . . . **fainted**   f) restrain, reduce speed
7. . . . . **brake**   g) dizzy, pass out, black out

8. . . . . **slow down**   h) anticipate, give the best guess about the climate

9. . . . . **swerve**   i) postpone, put off, reschedule

10. . . . . **steering wheel**   j) conditions dealing with poor health

11. . . . . **run away bus**   k) traveler, train or bus user

12. . . . . **popular**   l) a problem with the railway that recks the train

Exercise #5—Anagrams—Unscramble the words below and write a sentence.

- revesw_____ . . . .
. . . .
- alicdme_____ . . . .
. . . .
- intaf_____ . . . .
. . . .
- rabek_____ . . . .
. . . .
- upoparl_____ . . . .
. . . .
- ngieerts _____ . . . .
. . . .
- hleew_____ . . . .
. . . .
- socmumert _____ . . . .
. . . .

Exercise #6—Answer the following Wh-questions about the story:

❖ Who became a hero at his school? Why? _____
_____
_____

❖ What happened to the driver of the school bus? _____
_____

❖ Where did this story happen? What do you know about that place? ___
_____

❖ Where did Albi bring the bus to a stop? _____
_____

❖ Why did the bus driver faint? _____
_____

❖ What do you think of Albi's deed? _____
_____

❖ Who is your hero? How does he or she inspire you? _____
_____
_____

Exercise #7—Main idea: Which is the main idea of this story? Choose one of the following suggestions.

❖ A driver can faint while driving. This is the main idea because . . . .
. . . .
. . . .
. . . .

❖ The bad weather causes many accidents. This is the main idea because . . . .
. . . .
. . . .
. . . .

❖ Heroes are among us and they save many lives. This is the main idea because . . . .
. . . .
. . . .

Grammar Focus: Articles

INDEFINITE ARTICLE—**A** & **AN**

DEFINITE ARTICLE—**THE**

Study this example and read the explanation in the two boxes that follow:

I had **a** sandwich and **an** apple for lunch.	**The** sandwich was very fresh and the apple was very sweet.

The speaker says, "a" sandwich and"an" apple because this is the first time he talks about "apple" and "sandwich" in his sentence and the reader does not know anything about them.
 	
    We use "a" before a noun that starts with a consonant, ex: a boy, a book; we use "an" before a noun that starts with a vowel, ex: an apple, an elephant.
	Now the speaker says "the" before the noun "sandwich" because "sandwich" was mentioned before in the first sentence and the speaker knows something about the noun "sandwich".
	
	    We do not use any article before Proper Nouns.

 Exercise #8—Use the articles correctly with words that start with vowels or consonants. Write another sentence for each example.

 This is **an a**pple. Give other examples with letter **A**:

_____

This is **a b**anana. Give other examples with letter **B**:

_____

This is **a c**oat. Give other examples with letter **C**:

_____

This is **a d**ress. Give other examples with **D**:

_____

This is **an e**gg. Give other examples with letter **E**:

_____

This is **an i**ce cream. Give other examples with letter **I**:

_____

This is **an o**range. Give other examples with letter **O**:

_____

This is **an u**mbrella. Give other examples with letter **U**:

_____

Exercise #9: *Pair-work*—Let's learn how to use articles properly. Find nouns in the story "Town Hero". Divide them in two columns that start with vowels and consonants. Look at the article.

Article	Nouns that start with vowels	Nouns that start with consonants

Homework:—Fill in the blanks with the correct articles.

I am from Calgary, Alberta, ___ province of Canada. Calgary is ___ city in ___ Alberta. Alberta is not far from ___ north border of ___ United States. I live in ___ area called ___ Forest Lawn, which is on ___ South of ___ Calgary. I live in ___ house on ___ street in ___ South of ___ city. ___ street is called "Bear Street" and ___ house is old, more than 100 years old! I am ___ English teacher at ___ school in ___ center of ___ town. I like reading ___ books and taking ___ photographs. I usually go ___ home by ___ car. I usually have ___ lunch at school during my lunch break. We enjoy all kinds of ethnic foods in ___ Calgary. I like ___ Italian food very much. Sometimes, I go to ___ Italian restaurant near my school. ___ restaurant is called "Luigi's". ___ Italian food is great!

Supplemental reading: REQUIRED—Carefully read the following article about a heroic act and write your personal response in your reading log.

River rescue was truly heroic act[3]

Last Friday Riverview and Moncton firefighters and rescue teams, including an assist from the RCMP[4] and its helicopter, performed a daring and dangerous rescue of a woman who had fallen into the freezing and ice-choked waters of the Petitcodiac River. Particular mention of Riverview firefighter Troy Boomer, who leaped 20 feet from the police helicopter into the water to reach the woman, is merited. It was his job, but it was still an example of incredible heroics considering the circumstances and dangers. He literally risked his own life to save another; to do a job that every day can involve risk to one's own life. In addition, while Mr. Boomer deserves the praise and commendation, we are sure he would also be the first to say that his colleagues on the fire and rescue squad would all have done the same thing; that he was the one who happened to be called upon that particular day for that particular task. And it is true. For our firefighters and rescue teams are all well trained and train throughout the year to deal with all kinds of emergencies such as this one. And each one is ready to spring into action when necessary. One day it may be Mr. Boomer who plays the important role in getting the job done; another day it may be somebody else on the team.

The role of our firefighters has become remarkable from the days when they usually responded to house or building fires, although that remains an essential part of their job. And every time they do respond, the public witnesses these men demonstrating their bravery, entering burning structures to help put the blaze out, to check to ensure nobody is inside, and to rescue anybody who may be inside and unable to get out on their own. They all do it, every day. That is in itself heroism. The fact it is their job and that they get paid for it makes no difference to the remarkable fact: we can think of no others who put their personal safety on the line so obviously and so often. They do so without much fanfare and, often, with little real public recognition. The river rescue last Friday is a good example of that; it demonstrates the high level of training, skills and, yes, courage our firefighters possess and demonstrate virtually every day. They are indeed among today's true heroes.

---

[3]   Published Wednesday January 2nd, 2008. Appeared on page D4—Retrieved on February 3, 2008 from http://timestranscript.canadaeast.com/rss/article/171665

[4]   Royal Canadian Mounted Police

Independent work—Choose one of the two options:

A. Prepare a power point about a heroic deed. Make sure to describe your hero and what he or she did. Create a powerpoint that consists of 5 slides. Follow the steps below.
   1. Create a cover slide
   2. Describe the event
   3. Describe the person
   4. Describe the significance of the event to you
   5. What is the lesson you learned from the event?
   6. The content in the slides must be concise
   7. Use font Times Roman size 14.
   8. Use slide transition and animation of your choice in your presentation.
   9. Use new words you learned in this lesson and underline them in the slides
   10. Prepare to present the Power Point in class.

B. Write a personal response about the lessons you learned in this unit or about a heroic act you know about. Your response should consist of at least three paragraphs, have clear information, choose interesting facts and transitions for your paragraphs, get ready to present your ideas in class.

Study

STUDY TIP—Create a visual personal vocabulary log: Draw an image of a new vocabulary word or create a concept map of a word with synonyms, opposites, images, scenes, etc

SPOT THE MISTAKE—Find the mistakes and fix them. Write the correct sentence:

This teacher 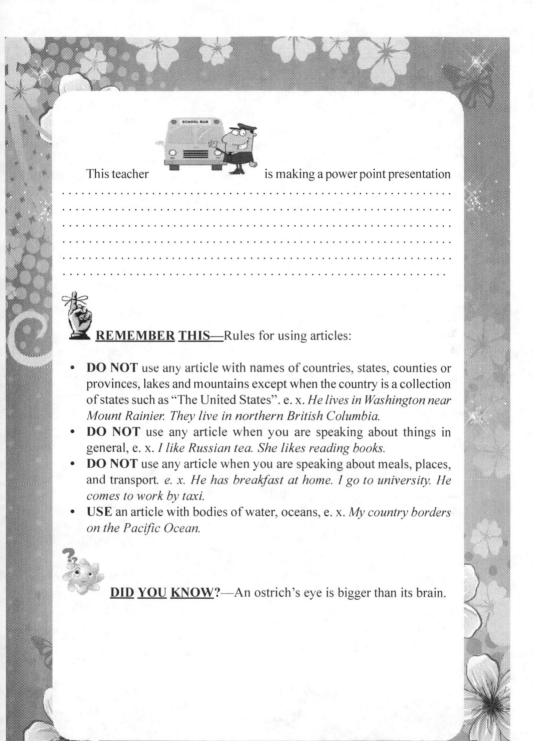 is making a power point presentation

. . . .
. . . .
. . . .
. . . .
. . . .
. . . .

REMEMBER THIS—Rules for using articles:

- **DO NOT** use any article with names of countries, states, counties or provinces, lakes and mountains except when the country is a collection of states such as "The United States". e. x. *He lives in Washington near Mount Rainier. They live in northern British Columbia.*
- **DO NOT** use any article when you are speaking about things in general, e. x. *I like Russian tea. She likes reading books.*
- **DO NOT** use any article when you are speaking about meals, places, and transport. *e. x. He has breakfast at home. I go to university. He comes to work by taxi.*
- **USE** an article with bodies of water, oceans, e. x. *My country borders on the Pacific Ocean.*

DID YOU KNOW?—An ostrich's eye is bigger than its brain.

LANGUAGE BANK—In this lesson you learned:

Active words	Recycled words	Passive words
1. tracks	1. classmate	1. firefighter
2. derailment	2. difficult	2. rescue
3. commuters	3. improve	3. assisst
4. announce	4. dramatically	4. freezing
5. major	5. weekend	5. ice-choked
6. weather	6. ride	6. helicopter
7. headache	7. usual	7. perform
8. safe	8. understand	8. daring
9. delay	9. due to	9. particular
10. throughout	10. climate	10. mention
11. faint	11. health	11. merited
12. extreme	12. condition	12. leap
13. swerve	13. danger	13. incredible
14. fast	14. decision	14. circumstances
15. rush	15. push	15. literally
16. region	16. sick	16. risk
17. contribute	17. cause	17deserve
18. accident	18. dangerous	18. praise
19. driveway	19. distinguish	19. commendation
20. deed	20. team	20. particular
21. centimeter	21. include	21. emergency
22. combine (with . . .)		22. respond
23. block		
24. railway		
25. service		
26. crash		
27. hero		
28. driver		
29. wheel		
30. rush		

Expressions: weather forecast, brought to a safe stop, run away bus, get hurt, steering wheel, brake pedal, slow down

31. street
32. icy
33. frozen
34. instantly
35. turn
36. examine
37. conclude
38. act

Lesson #2—Vote of Confidence

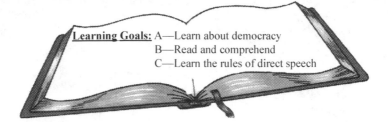

Learning Goals: A—Learn about democracy
B—Read and comprehend
C—Learn the rules of direct speech

Language Focus: Parts of speech

Context Clues—Pre-Reading: Check your vocabulary knowledge. Fill in the circle before the word with the same meaning as the bold word in the sentence.

❖ This issue is **significant** for the future of education. **"significant"** means:

    O seeing the future with an open mind
    O have a major or important effect
    O have special knowledge about an issue
    O teach people how to behave at school

❖ Students visited the **parliament** and met with the members of the House of Commons to learn more about the way democracy works. **"parliament"** means:

    O speaking to a group of people in a foreign language
    O trying to understand the way democracy works
    O a body of elected individuals who represent the people
    O the government makes decisions that help people

❖ A group of friends **nominated** her for the Distinguished Student Award. **"nominate"** means:

○ suggest that somebody be elected to a position of honour
○ his name comes from a word related to the stars
○ the best student in my class received a great award
○ teachers recognized Jim for his hard work

❖ His mother was a well-educated **journalist** and is very involved in politics. **"journalist"** means:

○ it is interesting to understand why she has a journal
○ she starts her day by reading a newspaper
○ my younger sister works for a television station
○ a writer for a newspaper or television station

Before you read, look at the picture and answer these questions:

1. Have you ever expressed your opinion on an important issue in your life? Describe your experience: _____
   _____
   _____
   _____

2. What do you know about the democratic election process in Canada?
   _____
   _____
   _____

3. Why is voting such an important civic responsibility for a Canadian citizen? _____
   _____
   _____
   _____

4. Are women well represented in the government in this country? Why?
_____
_____
_____

5. What do you know about women elected in the government of Canada? Find data. _____
_____
_____

6. Name and describe one of the main characteristics of democracy. ____
_____
_____
_____

7. What does the concept "equal rights" mean to you? Provide examples.
_____
_____
_____
_____

Vote of confidence

Women **representation** and their service to Canadians has been a **significant** **issue** in Canadian **politics**. The first woman, Agnes Macphail, was **elected** to the Canadian **House of Commons** in the 1921 **election**. **Although** **female** representation in politics has **increased** since then, and many political **parties** have increased the number of female **candidates** as an **organizational** and **political** goal, no major Canadian political party **to date** has **achieved** **gender** **parity** in the number of candidates **nominated** for election. Recently, the province of Alberta has distinguished itself in this field when it announced that the **main** political parties in the province are led by women. This fact contributes to gender parity in politics. However, in most of the provinces women representation is poor. This is seen in the fact that although more than half of Canadians are women, only 21 percent (21%) of our Members of Parliament are females.

Dr. Rosemary Speirs, a **retired journalist**, is **determined** to improve this situation. She stresses: "It is important to get women's **perspectives** into politics, to have their voices heard and to work with men as **partners**." "It would make for a stronger **democracy**", she concludes.

At 67, Dr. Speirs puts her **fair share** of **pressure** on political parties through *Equal Voice*, an organization which she founded in 2001 after retiring from her nearly 40-year political journalism **career**. "Women in Western democracies have made **tremendous gains in terms of** personal freedom and **financial security**," she says. However, she **maintains**, "It is important that women **secure** political power here."[5] **According to** *Equal Voice*, in women representation Canada **ranks** 46 out of 186 countries in the number of women who are elected to **national parliament**. Canada has elected fewer women to **federal government** than Rwanda, Iraq and Afghanistan. Although the female **population** in Canada is more than 52%, only 22% of the **members** of the House of Commons are women and only 21 % of the elected **municipal, provincial,** and federal government representatives are women. These facts are extreme and should be examined.

The **under-representation** of women in the Canadian political system has been well documented by **academics**, parliament and **the media**. **Despite** a 2004 **poll conducted** by the Centre for Research and Information on Canada, **stating** that 90 per cent of Canadians want more women elected, the representation of women in the House of Commons has reached a **plateau** of 20.8 per cent with only 64 women sitting as Members of Parliaments. **Similarly**, the **glass ceiling** for women in municipal and provincial governments **hovers** around 21 per cent. "Equal Voice" is a non-profit organization which aims to **change the face** of Canadian politics by **facilitating** the election of more women at all **levels** of government. We need to act and to act fast to change this situation.

---

[5]   Adapted from "Vote of Confidence" by Laurie Mackenzie; Canadian Living March 2008 pg. 24

Practice Your Knowledge

<u>**Exercise** #1</u>—Vocabulary study

Task 1—Check the meaning of the following words in your dictionary. Copy the definitions.

Task 2— Find the sentence with the same word from the text and copy it or write your own sentence. Follow the example with the word **"percent"**:

Definition—as expressed in hundredths, one hundredth part of something.

Sentence—A hundred <u>percent</u> of the students passed the test.

➢ Members of Parliament
Definition . . . .
. . . .
Sentence . . . .
. . . .

➢ determined
Definition . . . .
. . . .
Sentence . . . .
. . . .

➢ significant
Definition . . . .
. . . .
Sentence . . . .
. . . .

➢ issue
Definition . . . .
. . . .
Sentence . . . .
. . . .

➢ representation
Definition . . . .
. . . .
Sentence . . . .
. . . .
➢ important
Definition . . . .
. . . .
Sentence . . . .
. . . .
➢ elect
Definition . . . .
. . . .
Sentence . . . .
. . . .
➢ increase
Definition . . . .
. . . .
Sentence . . . .
. . . .
➢ perspectives
Definition . . . .
. . . .
Sentence . . . .
. . . .
➢ politics
Definition . . . .
. . . .
Sentence . . . .
. . . .
➢ gender
Definition . . . .
. . . .
Sentence . . . .
. . . .

➢ parity
Definition . . . .
. . . .
Sentence . . . .
. . . .

➢ nominate
Definition . . . .
. . . .
Sentence . . . .
. . . .

➢ democracy
Definition . . . .
. . . .
Sentence . . . .
. . . .

➢ candidate
Definition . . . .
. . . .
Sentence . . . .
. . . .

➢ founded
Definition . . . .
. . . .
Sentence . . . .
. . . .

➢ to be determined
Definition . . . .
. . . .
Sentence . . . .
. . . .

➢ fair share
Definition . . . .
. . . .
Sentence . . . .
. . . .

➢ journalism
Definition . . . .
. . . .
Sentence . . . .
. . . .

➢ career
Definition . . . .
. . . .
Sentence . . . .
. . . .

➢ tremendous
Definition . . . .
. . . .
Sentence . . . .
. . . .

➢ gain
Definition . . . .
. . . .
Sentence . . . .
. . . .

➢ in terms of
Definition . . . .
. . . .
Sentence . . . .
. . . .

➢ personal freedom
Definition . . . .
. . . .
Sentence . . . .
. . . .

➢ financial security
Definition . . . .
. . . .
Sentence . . . .
. . . .

➢ secure

Definition . . . .

. . . .

Sentence . . . .

. . . .

➢ political power

Definition . . . .

. . . .

Sentence . . . .

. . . .

➢ pressure

Definition . . . .

. . . .

Sentence . . . .

. . . .

➢ political

Definition . . . .

. . . .

Sentence . . . .

. . . .

➢ retire

Definition . . . .

. . . .

Sentence . . . .

. . . .

➢ municipal

Definition . . . .

. . . .

Sentence . . . .

. . . .

➢ federal

Definition . . . .

. . . .

Sentence . . . .

. . . .

➢ provincial

Definition . . . .
. . . .

Sentence . . . .
. . . .

➢ media

Definition . . . .
. . . .

Sentence . . . .
. . . .

➢ conduct

Definition . . . .
. . . .

Sentence . . . .
. . . .

➢ poll

Definition . . . .
. . . .

Sentence . . . .
. . . .

➢ plateau

Definition . . . .
. . . .

Sentence . . . .
. . . .

➢ glass ceiling

Definition . . . .
. . . .

Sentence . . . .
. . . .

Exercise #2: VOCABULARY BUILDING—Insert the right word from the list in the blanks. The sentences are taken from the text "A Vote of Confidence".

Members of Parliament	determined	perspectives
important	politics	democracy
journalism	tremendous	
percent	personal freedom	financial security

1. "It is _____ to get women's _____ into _____, to have their voices heard and to work with men as partners," she says.
2. Rosemary Speirs is _____ to change that.
3. More than half of Canadians are women, but only 21 _____ of our _____ are females.
4. It would make for a stronger _____.
5. Women in Western democracies have made _____ gains "in terms of" _____ _____ and _____ _____," she says.

Exercise #3: VOCABULARY BUILDING—New words used in a new context. Insert the right word from the list in the blanks. The sentences are not taken from the text but the words are used in the same meaning. Work with a friend:

Members of Parliament	political power	perspectives	important
democracy	career	in terms of	tremendous
personal freedom	financial security		

1. Many peoples of Africa are fighting for _____.
2. Since she was employed in the petroleum company, she is enjoying _____ _____.
3. Different community members gave their _____ on the new train station incident.
4. It is _____ to learn the new culture as we learn a new language.
5. Moving to a foreign country is a _____ change for both adults and young children.
6. Women in Canada are requiring more _____ _____.
7. My grandfather had a very successful _____.

8. A delegation of _____ ___ _____ went to visit the Canadian soldiers in Afghanistan.
9. ____ _____ ___job security, Calgary has become the best city to live in.

Exercise #4: VOCABULARY BUILDING—Match the words below with the definitions in the box.

1. . . . . . . **Members of Parliament**
2. . . . . . . **determined**
3. . . . . . . **political**
4. . . . . . . **power**
5. . . . . . . **perspectives**
6. . . . . . . **important**

7. . . . . . . **politics**
8. . . . . . . **democracy**

9. . . . . . . **founded**
10. . . . . . . **journalism**
11. . . . . . . **career**
12. . . . . . . **tremendous**
13. . . . . . . **secure**
14. . . . . . . **financial**
15. . . . . . . **security**

a) guarantee, protection
b) economic, related to money
c) confident, steady, dependable
d) job, profession, line of business
e) marvelous, wonderful, incredible
f) newspaper writing, reporting for TV station
g) established, created, started
h) supporting a party, following a group
i) point of view, picture,
j) central, significant, crucial
k) social equality, classlessness
l) strong-minded, firm,
m) government, principles
n) authority, influence, strength
o) representatives in the elected assembly

Exercise #5—Anagrams—Unscramble the words below and use them in sentences.

• entliaparm_____ . . . .
. . . .
. . . .

- ermbme_____ . . . .
. . . .
. . . .
- wreop_____ . . . .
. . . .
. . . .
- itcalopi_____ . . . .
. . . .
. . . .
- opranttmi_____ . . . .
. . . .
. . . .
- omracycde_____ . . . .
. . . .
. . . .
- suodnemert_____ . . . .
. . . .
. . . .
- nnaliaifc_____ . . . .
. . . .
. . . .
- rreace_____ . . . .
. . . .
. . . .

Exercise #6: Answer the following Wh-questions about the story:

1. Who is Rosemary Speirs? Give all the details you can find about her in the story. _____
_____
_____

2. How many women are members of the Canadian Parliament? _____
_____
_____
_____

3. What was Speirs' job? What do you know about that profession? ___
   _____
   _____

4. What is she fighting for now that she is retired? _____
   _____
   _____
   _____

5. What do you think is Equal Voice as an organization? _____
   _____
   _____
   _____

Exercise #7 : Main idea   Which is the main idea of this story? Choose one of the following and give the reasons for your choice.

❖ Equal rights are important in Canada. This is the main idea because
   . . . .
   . . . .
   . . . .

❖ The Canadian Parliament should increase the number of women in politics. This is the main idea because . . . .
   . . . .
   . . . .
   . . . .

❖ Women and men are born equal. This is the main idea because . . . .
   . . . .
   . . . .
   . . . .

Grammar Focus: We often have to give information about what people say or think. In order to do this you can use direct or quoted speech, or indirect or reported speech. The **direct (quoted) speech**: *"I like it," he said. "Irene is late," he thought. "I will pass the exam," she hoped.* The **indirect (reported) speech**: *He said he liked it. He thought that Irene was late. She hoped she would pass the exam.*

The direct (quoted) speech is typically introduced by verbs such as *say, tell, admit, complain, explain, remind, reply, think, hope, offer, refuse* etc. If the verbs before the quotation marks are in the past tense, we change the following when we write indirect (reported) speech:

a) We change the **verb tenses** in the following way:
    1. Present tense to past tense: *"I never <u>understand</u> you,"* she told me. *She told me she never <u>understood</u> me.*
    2. Present perfect tense—past perfect tense: *"I <u>have broken</u> the window,"* he admitted. *He admitted that he <u>had broken</u> the window.*
    3. Past tense—past perfect tense: *"She <u>went</u> to Rome,"* I thought. *I thought that she <u>had gone</u> to Rome.*

b) **pronouns change**: *She said: <u>I</u> study English online. She said <u>she</u> studies English online.*

c) the **adverbs of time and place**—If the reported sentence contains an expression of time, you must change it to fit in with the time of reporting.

this (evening)	›	that (evening)
today	›	yesterday . . .
these (days)	›	those (days)
now	›	then
(a week) ago	›	(a week) before
last weekend	›	the weekend before last / the previous weekend
here	›	there
next (week)	›	the following (week)
tomorrow	›	the next/following day

Exercise #8—Choose the correct form to change the following sentences from direct into indirect speech. Fill in the circle with the correct answer.

1. "I got the message while I was waiting at the bus stop." He told me that

○ he got the message while he was waiting at the bus stop
○ he had got the message while he had been waiting at the bus stop

2. "We will set off tomorrow." They said
○ they would set off the next day
○ they would set off tomorrow

3. "Get out of my way!" He ordered us
○ to get out of his way
○ we got out of his way

4. "I invited him last week." She told me this week that
○ she invited him the previous week
○ she invited him last week

5. "I will resign today." This morning he announced that he
○ would resign today
○ would resign that day

6. "We used to take the same medicine." She thought that
○ they had used to take the same medicine
○ they used to take the same medicine

7. "I entered the university a year ago." He told me last year
○ he had entered the university a year before
○ he had entered the university a year ago

8. "It is time we had an agreement." She suggested that
○ it was time that we had had an agreement
○ it was time we had an agreement

9. "We must go skiing in winter." He said that
○ they must go skiing in winter
○ they had to go skiing in winter

Homework—There are two cases of direct speech in the story 'Vote of Confidence'. Find them a change them into indirect speech.

1. . . . .
   . . . .
   . . . .
   . . . .
2. . . . .
   . . . .
   . . . .
   . . . .

Supplemental reading: REQUIRED—Carefully read the following letter that Dr. Rosemary Speirs wrote to Prime Minister of Canada, Mr. Jean Chretien. Write your own letter to a government representative or the school administrator regarding a problem you see in your school or city. Follow the model of Dr. Speirs' letter and explain clearly: *What is the problem? *Why is it so important to you?* What do you propose? *How is it going to change the situation?

Dr. Rosemary Speirs IN THE NEWS *January 28, 2002*
Rosemary Speirs
Equal Voice
116 Albert, Suite 810
Ottawa, Ontario K1P 5G3

Letter to: The Rt. Hon. Jean Chretien
Prime Minister's Office
Langevin Block,
80 Wellington St.,
Ottawa, Ont. K1A 0A2

Dear Mr. Chretien:
 We were astonished by the newspaper accounts of your exchange with Dr. Carolyn Bennett, chair of the Liberal women's caucus, over the issue of the number of women in your cabinet. If you really

suggested that she should not have aired the issue in public, we wish to vehemently disagree. We are a group of about 60 women, some elected, some active in the three national political parties, some in professional life, some students, who are all united by our belief that Canada needs more elected women. We deplore the failure of all political parties, not just yours, to promote and support equality for women interested in running for public office in Canada.

We're calling on you as prime minister and leader of the Liberal Party of Canada, to support reforms that would permit more interested women to be elected. We don't think you should be quashing an elected member of your government who bravely attempts to raise the issue. Your recent shuffle downgraded the women's issue portfolio, reduced the number of women in cabinet, dropped two women ministers and brought only one into the inner circle that governs the country.

We understand that you rightfully pride yourself on the number of women you have appointed to run as MPs, to sit in the Senate, on the Supreme Court and other federal bodies. We give you full credit for these welcome efforts to promote women. But we'd point out that your party's record in nominating women would have been dismal without your intervention. In 1993, there would have been no Liberal woman candidate in Metro Toronto and in 1997 only two.

Appointment is just a stop gap measure. For the longer term, party nomination procedures which systematically work to exclude women need to be changed. A simple reform would be strict limits on nomination spending. Women rarely have access to the same networks as men, so the big money requirements of contesting an urban Liberal nomination remain a huge barrier. For the women's movement, the parties' failure to promote more women in political life has proved a huge disappointment. In the Seventies and Eighties, we saw real progress and believed that women would take their place alongside men as the lawmakers and leaders of the country. Instead, in the 1990s, progress stalled. The number of women elected remained static while the number of women getting nominated has actually declined.

Women who want to take part in political life bump against a glass ceiling of about 20 per cent. We are permitted somewhere between a fifth and a quarter of the Commons. Parliament remains a mostly male club. Your cabinet reflects the Liberal party's general failure to treat women as equals. Talented Liberal women politicians have, and do, hold major portfolios in your government. But, as in the party, and in

Parliament, women can't seem to break through a system which denies them parity. The discrimination built into politics reflects adversely on all Canadian women. The situation cries out for reform, both within political parties, and without. We believe Parliament should be studying a more equitable electoral system than the outmoded riding-based electoral system we have now, which serves only to reproduce the status quo, and exclude so many Canadians of lesser means, not just women.

We, also, believe you should be pinning medals on Dr. Bennett for championing the cause of more women in politics. She's worked hard to encourage young women to consider political careers, and is recognized for her efforts by women in all parties. Far from airing laundry in public, she has improved the Liberal party's image. So has Heritage Minister Sheila Copps, and the other Liberal women Members and Cabinet Ministers who have over the years lent their support publicly and privately to the cause of electing more women.

We recognize that you want the Liberal party to be an open organization, welcoming to all comers. We're asking you to turn that personal commitment into a formal Liberal party policy, and into a government policy. We'd like to see the cause of getting more women elected moving forward, not stalled, during your long and successful term as Prime Minister of Canada.

Yours truly,
Rosemary Speirs
Chair

Study

STUDY TIP—Do not read a story word-by-word, or translate word-by-word. Prepare yourself for a reading: study its vocabulary first; review the pre-reading questions. Then put aside everything and just read, even twice. Do not look up vocabulary while reading.

SPOT THE MISTAKE—Find the mistakes and fix them. Write the correct sentence:

This woman   is elected to parliament for the first time . . . .

. . . .
. . . .
. . . .
. . . .
. . . .
. . . .

REMEMBER THIS—In English there are nouns which are used only in the plural. They are known as `pair nouns`, for example jeans, glasses, scissors, etc. If you want to refer to an exact number, use **a/one pair of**, like in the following example. I have bought **a/one pair of jeans**. I have bought **two pairs of jeans**.

DID YOU KNOW?—Lemons contain more sugar than strawberries.

LANGUAGE BANK—In this lesson you learned:

Active words	**Recycled words**	**Passive words**
1. representation	1. major	1. message
2. significant	2. service	2. set off
3. issue	3. announce	3. previous
4. politics	4. extreme	4. resign
5. elect	5. contribute	5. agreement
6. election	6. examine	6. skiing
7. although	7. conclude	7. administrator
8. female	8. act	8. regard
9. increase	9. province	9. model
10. party	10. distinguished	10. propose
11. to date	11. improve	11. astonished
12. achieve	12. situation	12. account
13. gender	13. stress	13. exchange
14. parity	14. important	14. cabinet
15. nominate	15. however	15. vehemently
16. main	16. representative	16. failure
17. retired	17. circle	17. public
18. journalist	18. invite	18. prime minister
19. determine	19. medicine	19. permit
20. perspective	20. enter	20. bravely
21. partner	21. situation	21. shuffle
22. democracy	22. belief	22. portfolio
23. pressure	23. dismal	
24. career	24. appoint	
25. tremendous	25. promote	
26. gains	26. intervention	
27. financial		
28. security		
29. maintain		
30. secure		

31. to rank
32. national
33. federal
34. provincial
35. parliament
36. government
37. population
38. municipal
39. under-representation
40. academics
41. media
42. despite
43. poll
44. conduct
45. to state
46. plateau
47. hover
48. facilitate
49. level

Expressions: House of Commons, fare share, in terms of, reach a plateau, according to, glass ceiling, change the face of . . . .

Lesson #3—A Marathon of Hope

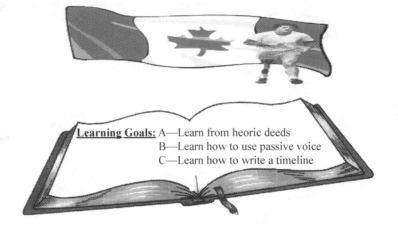

Learning Goals: A—Learn from heoric deeds
B—Learn how to use passive voice
C—Learn how to write a timeline

Language Focus: Passive Voice

Language Focus: Story Timeline

Context Clues—Pre-Reading: Check your vocabulary knowledge. Fill in the circle before the word with the same meaning as the bold word in the sentence.

❖ His parents raised him to appreciate his **integrity**. **"integrity"** means:

     O achieving high standards in the pre-Olympic games
     O work hard to meet the requirements for high school graduation
     O the quality of possessing high moral and professional standards
     O people hold her to high standards as a famous athlete

❖ Our soccer team displayed a great **athletic** attitude in the game. **"athletic"** means:

O things related to athletes or sports activities
O boys who participate in the soccer team
O competition organized annually
O she is considered a famous athlete

❖ Doctors made the difficult decision to **amputate** her arm due to cancer. **"amputate"** means:

O the doctor gave him medicine
O nurses take good care of their patients
O she was diagnosed with lung cancer
O cut off a part of the body

❖ They organized a spring **marathon** to raise funds for schools in Africa. **"marathon"** means:

O to participate in Olympic games
O to become a distinguished athlete
O a long distance running race
O a decision to play hockey

❖ She had smoked all her life and had her **lung** removed due to cancer. **"lung"** means:

O an activity that helps the body stay healthy
O a body organ that transfers oxygen into the blood
O the quality of producing new blood to the body
O people who suffer from a blood disease

Before you read, look at the picture in the previous page and answer these questions:

1. Do you know the young man in the picture? What do you know about him? _____
_____
_____
_____

2. Have you ever had a life threatening illness or do you know anybody with a life threatening disease? Describe the experience. _____

_____

_____

3. Do you know anybody who has survived a life threatening illness? Tell us about him or her. _____

_____

_____

4. What do you think is the most difficult part of dealing with a serious illness?_____

_____

_____

5. Do you know anybody who has turned the pain into strength to go on? Tell us about him or her. _____

_____

_____

_____

Read the story and answer the questions that follow:

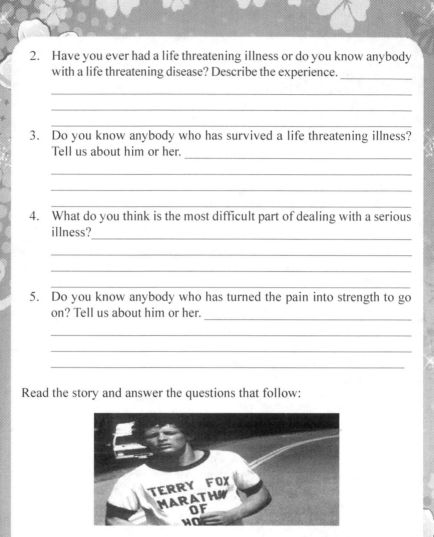

A Marathon of Hope

Terry Fox was born in Winnipeg, Manitoba, and was **raised** in Port Coquitlam, a small town in British Columbia, on the west coast of Canada. He was a very active and **athletic** young man. Terry was involved in many sports. At the **tender age** of 18 years old, he was **diagnosed** with a dangerous disease, **"estrogenic sarcoma"** (**bone cancer**). Terry was **forced** to have his right leg **amputated** 15 centimeters above the **knee** in 1977.

During the time Terry was **hospitalized**, he **witnessed** the **suffering** of other cancer **patients**, especially young children. After Terry lost his leg to cancer, he learned that **funding** for cancer research in Canada was very **limited**. That **motivated** Terry for his *Marathon of Hope* **to raise funds** to help find a **cure** for cancer. Although **seriously** sick, he decided to run across Canada to raise money for cancer research. His **journey** was called the *Marathon of Hope.* Terry spent eighteen months of **preparation** and running over 5,000 kilometers to get ready for the Marathon of Hope.

Terry started his **marathon** in St. John's, Newfoundland on April 12, 1980. At the beginning nobody **paid much attention** to Terry's run. However, **eventually** enthusiasm grew and the money that was **collected** along his **route** began **to mount**. He ran forty two kilometers a day through Canada's Atlantic Provinces, Quebec and Ontario. **Unfortunately**, on September 1, 1980, after 143 days and 5,373 **kilometers**, Terry was forced to stop his Marathon of Hope. This happened just outside of Thunder Bay, Ontario. The doctors examined him and decided to stop the marathon because cancer had **appeared** again, this time in his **lungs**.

Terry's journey was a journey that Canadians will never forget. An **entire nation** was **stunned** and **saddened** at the **shocking news** about Terry's health problems. Terry **passed away** on June 28, 1981 at age 22, but his **legacy lives on**. The heroic, young Canadian was gone, but his legacy was just beginning. To date, more than $400 million has been raised **worldwide** for cancer research in Terry's name through the **annual** Terry Fox Run held across Canada and around the world.

A special organization called "Terry Fox Foundation" was **created** in 1981. The Terry Fox Foundation **strives** to maintain the heroic **efforts** and **integrity** that Terry himself **embodied**. It is an organization that does not **seek** government funding for **administration** or fundraising **costs** other than small **grants** for **temporary**, part-time help. The first annual Terry Fox Run in 1981 was organized in Canada. However, many countries have joined The Terry Fox Run since then. All money raised in Terry's name is **distributed** through the National Cancer Institute of Canada. For those who knew Terry Fox and for those who only know of him, today Terry Fox continues to **inspire** thousands of people around the world three **decades** after the Marathon of Hope.

Practice Your Knowledge

Exercise **#1**—Vocabulary study

Task 1—Check the meaning of the following words in your dictionary. Copy the definitions.

Task 2—Find the sentence with the same word from the text and copy it or write your own sentence. Follow the example with the word **"raise"**:

Definition—act as a parent to somebody

Sentence—After her husband died young, Mrs. Brown raised her children all by herself.

➢ diagnose

Definition . . . .
. . . .
Sentence . . . .
. . . .

➢ to force

Definition . . . .
. . . .
Sentence . . . .
. . . .

➢ amputate

Definition . . . .
. . . .
Sentence . . . .
. . . .

➢ kilometer

Definition . . . .
. . . .
Sentence . . . .
. . . .

➢ to witness
Definition . . . .
. . . .
Sentence . . . .
. . . .
➢ entire
Definition . . . .
. . . .
Sentence . . . .
. . . .
➢ stun
Definition . . . .
. . . .
Sentence . . . .
. . . .
➢ sadden
Definition . . . .
. . . .
Sentence . . . .
. . . .
➢ legacy
Definition . . . .
. . . .
Sentence . . . .
. . . .
➢ worldwide
Definition . . . .
. . . .
Sentence . . . .
. . . .
➢ annual
Definition . . . .
. . . .
Sentence . . . .
. . . .

➢ athletic

Definition . . . .

. . . .

Sentence . . . .

. . . .

➢ tender

Definition . . . .

. . . .

Sentence . . . .

. . . .

➢ age

Definition . . . .

. . . .

Sentence . . . .

. . . .

➢ bone

Definition . . . .

. . . .

Sentence . . . .

. . . .

➢ cancer

Definition . . . .

. . . .

Sentence . . . .

. . . .

➢ hospitalize

Definition . . . .

. . . .

Sentence . . . .

. . . .

➢ suffering

Definition . . . .

. . . .

Sentence . . . .

. . . .

➤ patient
Definition . . . .
. . . .
Sentence . . . .
. . . .
➤ funding
Definition . . . .
. . . .
Sentence . . . .
. . . .
➤ limited
Definition . . . .
. . . .
Sentence . . . .
. . . .
➤ motivate
Definition . . . .
. . . .
Sentence . . . .
. . . .
➤ cure
Definition . . . .
. . . .
Sentence . . . .
. . . .
➤ seriously
Definition . . . .
. . . .
Sentence . . . .
. . . .
➤ journey
Definition . . . .
. . . .
Sentence . . . .
. . . .

➢ marathon

Definition . . . .

. . . .

Sentence . . . .

. . . .

➢ eventually

Definition . . . .

. . . .

Sentence . . . .

. . . .

➢ collect

Definition . . . .

. . . .

Sentence . . . .

. . . .

➢ route

Definition . . . .

. . . .

Sentence . . . .

. . . .

➢ to mount

Definition . . . .

. . . .

Sentence . . . .

. . . .

➢ unfortunately

Definition . . . .

. . . .

Sentence . . . .

. . . .

➢ appear

Definition . . . .

. . . .

Sentence . . . .

. . . .

➢ lung
Definition . . . .
. . . .
Sentence . . . .
. . . .

➢ nation
Definition . . . .
. . . .
Sentence . . . .
. . . .

➢ to create
Definition . . . .
. . . .
Sentence . . . .
. . . .

➢ to strive
Definition . . . .
. . . .
Sentence . . . .
. . . .

➢ effort
Definition . . . .
. . . .
Sentence . . . .
. . . .

➢ integrity
Definition . . . .
. . . .
Sentence . . . .
. . . .

➢ embody
Definition . . . .
. . . .
Sentence . . . .
. . . .

➢ seek

Definition . . . .

. . . .

Sentence . . . .

. . . .

➢ administration

Definition . . . .

. . . .

Sentence . . . .

. . . .

➢ fundraising

Definition . . . .

. . . .

Sentence . . . .

. . . .

➢ cost

Definition . . . .

. . . .

Sentence . . . .

. . . .

➢ grant

Definition . . . .

. . . .

Sentence . . . .

. . . .

➢ temporary

Definition . . . .

. . . .

Sentence . . . .

. . . .

➢ distribute

Definition . . . .

. . . .

Sentence . . . .

. . . .

➢ inspire

Definition . . . .
. . . .
Sentence . . . .
. . . .

➢ decade

Definition . . . .
. . . .
Sentence . . . .
. . . .

Exercise #2: VOCABULARY BUILDING—Insert the right word from the list in the blanks. The sentences are taken from the text "A Marathon of Hope".

was forced	amputated	centimeters	involve
diagnose	dangerous	research	witnessed
paid (much) attention	stunned and saddened		young man
shocking news	passed away	legacy	annual

➢ Terry was . . . . to have his right leg . . . .
. . . . 15 . . . . above the knee in 1977.
➢ He was an active, athletic . . . . .who was . . . .
. . . . in many sports.
➢ When Terry was only 18 years old, he was . . . .
. . . . with a . . . . disease, "estrogenic sarcoma" (bone cancer).
➢ At that time he decided to run across Canada to raise money for cancer . . . .
➢ While he was in hospital, Terry . . . . the suffering of other cancer patients, especially young children.
➢ At the beginning nobody . . . .
. . . . to Terry's run.
➢ An entire nation was . . . . and . . . .
. . . . at the . . . .

➢ Terry . . . . on June 28, 1981 at age 22, but his . . . . lives on.

➢ To date, more than $400 million has been raised worldwide for cancer research in Terry's name through the . . . . Terry Fox Run held across Canada and around the world.

Exercise #3: VOCABULARY BUILDING—New words used in a new context. Insert the right word from the list in the blanks. The sentences are not taken from the text but the words are used in the same meaning. Work with a friend:

west coast	involve	diagnose	amputate	worldwide
centimeter	to witness	raise money	research	kilometer
annual	entire	stunned and saddened		legacy
shocking news		pass away	young man	

❑ Canadian soldiers are known . . . . .as peacekeepers.

❑ My teacher always uses the . . . . findings to improve our English proficiency.

❑ Terry Fox is well known . . . . for his bravery.

❑ My grandmother . . . . last month.

❑ I am . . . . in the drama production of "Ann of Green Gables".

❑ His arm was . . . . due to a car accident.

❑ Terry Fox's . . . . lives on in the hearts of Canadians, who continue to . . . . for cancer . . . .

❑ I finished the . . . . book in three days.

❑ How many . . . . .are there in a . . . .
. . . .?

❑ She was . . . . with a heart disease.

❑ My little brother was . . . .
. . . . because he . . . . .the little dog die.

❑ He heard the . . . . on TV last night.

❑ Her uncle lives in the . . . . of Canada.

❑ They participated in an . . . . competition.

Exercise #4: Answer the following Wh-questions about the story:

1. Where was Terry Fox born? ....
   ....

2. Where was he raised? ....
   ....

3. When did he get sick? ....
   ....

4. What was he diagnosed with? ....
   ....

5. What did the doctors do in 1977? ....
   ....

6. What did he witness when he was in hospital? ....
   ....

7. What is the Marathon of Hope? ....
   ....

8. How many days and kilometers did Terry run to prepare for the Marathon? ....
   ....

9. What is Terry's legacy? ....
   ....

10. How does Terry's legacy inspire you and others? ....
    ....

Exercise #5—Anagrams. Unscramble the words below and write sentences:

- aidgnodez_____ ....
  ....
- nigckohs_____ ....
  ....
- uattepam_____ ....
  ....

- olvevni_____ ·······························
·······························
- eearshcr_____ ·······························
·······························
- iesswtn_____ ·······························
·······························
- aaunnl_____ ·······························
·······························
- aeygcl_____ ·······························
·······························
- aeuodgnrs_____ ·······························
·······························

<u>Exercise #6:</u> **VOCABULARY BUILDING**—Match the words below with the definitions in the box.

1. . . . . . **diagnosed**	a) including everything, from beginning to end
2. . . . . . **shocking**	b) stop living, to come to an end
3. . . . . . **amputate**	c) identify an illness in a patient
4. . . . . . **involve**	d) provoking a deep emotional feeling
5. . . . . . **research**	e) include something as a necessary element
6. . . . . . **witness**	f) cut off part of a body with an operation
7. . . . . . **annual**	g) an organized study to find more facts
8. . . . . . **legacy**	h) happening once a year
9. . . . . . **dangerous**	i) somebody who sees an event
10. . . . . . **centimeter**	j) something that is left after somebody dies
11. . . . . . **pass away**	k) likely to cause injury or harm
12. . . . . . **entire**	l) a measurement equal to one hundredth of a meter

<u>**Grammar**</u> <u>Focus:</u> **Passive Voice** of the verbs is used when the focus is on the action not on the person who performs the action. Example: My bike **was stolen.** (it is not important and we do not know who stole

the bike but we focus on the fact that the bike was stolen). Terry Fox **was forced** to stop the Marathon of Hope because cancer appeared in his lungs. (we do not know and it is not important who stopped Terry Fox but the fact that Terry had to stop the Marathon of Hope)

Sometimes a statement in passive voice is considered more polite than a statement in active voice, as the following example shows: A mistake was made. In this case, the focus is on the fact that a mistake was made, but not to blame anyone (e.g. You made a mistake.)

How Passive Voice Is Formed

Subject + a form of the verb "to *be*" + Past Participle of the verb (regular verbs - verb+ed, 3rd column of irregular verbs)

Example: A letter + was + written. = Passive voice

When changing active sentences into passive voice, we must pay close attention to the following rules:

1. the object of the active sentence becomes the subject of the passive sentence. **I** write the **story.** The **story** is written (by **me**).
2. the form of the verb is changed (*to be* + past participle of regular verbs(or 3rd column of irregular verbs). E.x. **"write "** is changed into **"is written"**.
3. the subject of the active sentence becomes the object of the passive sentence (or is dropped altogether as it is not important).

Examples of Passive Voice—Simple Tenses

Tense		Subject	Verb	Object
Simple Present	*Active:*	Donna	writes	a letter.
	Passive:	A letter	is written	by Donna
Simple Past	*Active:*	Donna	wrote	a letter.
	Passive:	A letter	was written	by Donna.
Future	*Active:*	Donna	will write	a letter.
	Passive:	A letter	will be written	by Donna.
Present Progressive	*Active:*	Rita	is writing	a letter.
	Passive:	A letter	is being written	by Rita.

Past	*Active:*	Rita	was writing	a letter.
Progressive	*Passive:*	A letter	was being written	by Rita.
Present	*Active:*	Rita	has written	a letter.
Perfect	*Passive:*	A letter	has been written	by Rita.
Past	*Active:*	Rita	had written	a letter.
Perfect	*Passive:*	A letter	had been written	by Rita.
	Active:	Rita	will have written	a letter.
Future Perfect	*Passive:*	A letter	will have been written	by Rita.

Exercise #7: Form passive voice sentences from the following words using Simple Present of the verbs. You are given a noun and a verb (a subject and a predicate), form a sentence first in active voice and then change it into passive voice. Follow the example: **the documents / to print**

Active voice—The immigration officer printed the documents.
Passive voice—The documents were printed (by the immigration officer).

1. **the window / open**
Active voice _____
Passive voice _____
2. **the shoes / buy**
Active voice _____
Passive voice _____
3. **the car / wash**
Active voice _____
Passive voice _____
4. **the litter / throw away**
Active voice _____
Passive voice _____
5. **the letter / send**
Active voice _____
Passive voice _____
6. **the book / read / not**
Active voice _____

Passive voice _____
  7. **the songs / sing / not**
Active voice _____
Passive voice _____
  8. **the food / eat / not**
Active voice _____
Passive voice _____
  9. **the shop / close / not**
Active voice _____
Passive voice _____
  10. **the ball/throw away/ young player**
Active voice _____
Passive voice _____

Exercise #8: Rewrite the following sentences in passive voice.
E.x.: He opens the door.—The door is opened (by him).
1. We set the table. _____
2. She paid a lot of money. _____
3. I drew a picture. _____
4. They wore blue shoes. _____
5. They did not help you. _____
6. He did not read the book. _____
7. You did not write the letter. _____
8. Did your mother pick you up? _____
9. Did the police catch the thief? _____
10. The teacher was instructing the students. _____

Literature Focus—Story Timeline

Story timeline is a schedule of activities or events in a story; it is a kind of timetable. It gives a chronology of the events happening in a story. The timeline is a representation of key events within a particular story or historical period, often consisting of illustrative visual material accompanied by written commentary, arranged chronologically. Here is a story and a timeline: STORY—Maria's parents want to keep track of important things in her life. They decide to make a timeline. Maria was born in 1993. She walked for the first time in 1995, when she was two years old. The next year, she said her first words. In 1998, she celebrated her fifth birthday. Her parents can keep track of all these things by putting them on a timeline like the one below.

TIMELINE:

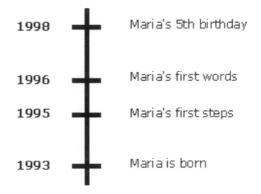

1998	Maria's 5th birthday
1996	Maria's first words
1995	Maria's first steps
1993	Maria is born

Exercise #9: Use the following steps to write a timeline about the life of Terry Fox. Follow these steps to prepare to create the timeline:

- ❑ First collect enough facts about Terry Fox's Marathon of Hope and about the cities and provinces through which he traveled. Use the internet or the library to collect the data.
- ❑ Check different sources and record the information to complete the timeline of Terry's story
- ❑ Trace Terry's journey on the map of Canada and write the information for each city in his journey.

Over each line of the Timeline, place one phrase that describes the actions and the times when they happened. Event #1 #2 #3 #4 #5 #6 #7 #8 #9 #10

- > **PREPARATIONS**—Terry Gets Ready: April 11, 1980 Terry Fox is ready for anything that may happen on the road.
- > **St. John Newfoundland Km #0** DAY 1: April 12, 1980 The Marathon of Hope begins.
- > **Eastern Newfoundland Km #18** DAY 2: April 13, 1980 CBC Radio's Sound of Sports begins regular coverage of Terry's run.
- > **Gambo, Newfoundland Km #306** DAY 9: April 20, 1980 One week into his run, Terry is interviewed from the road
- > **Corner Brook, Newfoundland Km #748** DAY 20: May 1, 1980 Terry speaks of his inspiration in this recently rediscovered television interview.
- > **Thunder Bay Ontario Km #5374** The end of the road: Sept. 2, 1980 A tearful Terry Fox discovers that his cancer has returned.

Exercise #10—Create a six slide power point presentation based on what you learned about Terry Fox. Your power point must consist of a cover slide and 5 content slides. The content in the slides must be concise and you must use font Times Roman size 14. Use slide transition and animation of your choice in your presentation. Prepare to present the Power Point in class. Use the new words you learned in this unit in your presentation and underline them in the slides. The following are some ideas you may write about:

- ❖ Who was Terry Fox?
- ❖ What happened to him?
- ❖ What did he achieve in his short life?
- ❖ How does Terry's life inspire you?

Homework: Read the story "A Marathon of Hope" again and identify all the verbs in Passive Voice. Write them down:

. . . .
. . . .
. . . .
. . . .

....
....
....
....
....
....
....
....
....

SPOT THE MISTAKE—Find the mistakes and fix them. Write the correct sentence:

The teacher is helping the student amputate his left arm. ....
....
....
....
....
....

240

DID YOU KNOW?—The names of all continents both start and end with the same letter. For example: America, Asia, Europe, etc.

 **LANGUAGE BANK**—In this lesson you learned:

Active words	Recycled words	Passive words
1. raise	1. young	1. instruct
2. athletic	2. invlove	2. identify
3. tender	3. dangerous	3. timetable
4. age	4. disease	4. schedule
5. diagnose	5. weast coast	5. chronology
6. bone	6. centimeter	6. particular
7. cancer	7. especially	7. historical
8. to force	8. research	8. illustrative
9. amputate	9. although	9. visual
10. hospitalize	10. sick	10. accompanied
11. to witness	11. accross	11. commentary
12. suffering	12. decide	12. arrange
13. patient	13. money	13. keep track
14. funding	14. get ready	
15. limited	15. nobody	
16. motivate	16. enthusiasm	
17. cure	17. however	
18. seriously	18. province	
19. journey	19. examine	
20. marathon	20. decide	
21. eventually	21. health	
22. collect	22. problem	
23. route	23. to date	
24. to mount to	24. special	
25. unfortunately	25. organization	

26. kilometers
27. appear
28. lung
29. entire
30. nation
31. stunned
32. saddened
33. legacy
34. worldwide
35. annual
36. create
37. strive
38. effort
39. integrity
40. embody
41. seek
42. administration
43. fundraising
44. cost
45. grant
46. temporary
47. distribute
48. inspire
49. decade

26. maintain
27. government
28. join
29. representation
30. consist of . . . .
31. important
32. celebrate

Expressions: estrogenic sarcoma, raise funds, pay attention to, shocking news, pass away, live on.

Lesson #4—A Doctor Without Borders

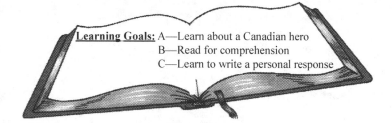

Learning Goals: A—Learn about a Canadian hero
B—Read for comprehension
C—Learn to write a personal response

Language Focus: Personal Response

Context Clues—Pre-Reading: Check your vocabulary knowledge. Fill in the circle before the word with the same meaning as the bold word in the sentence.

❖ Unfortunately, a large number of couples choose **divorce** as a solution. **"divorce"** means:

    O one of the best ways to lose weight and become active
    O the way the criminal is treated by the court officers
    O an ending of a marriage by an official decision of the court
    O two people in love decide to go on a trip in summer

❖ Teaching English in a structured way is **controversial** issue. **"controversial"** means:

    O strong disagreement or disapproval, e.g. in public debate
    O the teenager always disagrees with his parents and complains
    O the soccer coach makes decisions and the players must follow them
    O two people disagree about the kind of lifestyle they want to live

❖ My younger brother is a **surgeon** and enjoys his job very much.
  "surgeon" means:

  ○ one of the ways to treat patients
  ○ the nurse takes care of her patients
  ○ an doctor who looks after children
  ○ a doctor specializing in operations

❖ We donated blood last week as there are many patients who need
  blood **transfusion**. **"transfusion"** means:

  ○ an eye doctor treats his patients very well
  ○ the transfer of blood from a healthy donor into the patient
  ○ the new medication is helping the patient who had surgery
  ○ a doctor takes care of the new mother

❖ Mother Teresa was a best example of a **humanitarian** person.
  "humanitarian" means:

  ○ committed to improving the lives of other people
  ○ the way a teacher finds models of teaching her students
  ○ an endless improvement of language proficiency
  ○ two people who help each other in difficult situations

Before you read, look at the picture and answer these questions:

1. Do you know about anybody who has dedicated his or her life to
   people of other countries? _____
   _____
   _____

2. What kinds of medical specialists do you know besides your family
   doctor? _____
   _____
   _____

3. In what ways do doctors show their care and commitment to their patients? _____
_____
_____

4. What do you know about medical services in Canada? _____
_____
_____
_____

Read the story and answer the questions

Dr. Norman Bethune—The Famous Canadian

Norman Bethune (1890-1939) was born in Gravenhurst, Ontario. He **attended** the University of Toronto. In 1911, Bethune **interrupted** his studies in biology at the University of Toronto to work at Frontier College, **setting up** classes for immigrant workers in a bush **lumber** camp in northern Ontario. Then again his education was interrupted when he **enlisted** as a **stretcher bearer** in World War I. He received his Medical Doctor (M.D.) degree in 1916, when he returned from war.

Dr. Bethune became seriously sick and was diagnosed with **tuberculosis**. His wife, Frances, was determined to stay by his side, but Bethune **demanded** a **divorce** and sent Frances back to Scotland; Bethune had accepted his **inevitable** death, and didn't want to **waste** Frances' time. Even after their divorce, however, they **frequently** wrote to each other. Bethune had **given up on himself** but a letter from the Trudeau Sanatorium in New York changed his life. While at Trudeau Sanatorium, Bethune read about a new and **controversial** **treatment** for tuberculosis called **compression** **therapy**, or **artificial** pneumothorax (insertion of air into the chest so as to **collapse** one lung either **permanently** or temporarily depending on the case to let the other lung **recover**). Dr. Bethune demanded the compression therapy and received it. His left lung was compressed and he recovered and was cured.

Dr. Bethune left New York for Montreal to study thoracic **surgery**. From 1928 to 1936, Dr. Bethune worked as a thoracic **surgeon** in Montreal. He became famous there for his treatment of tuberculosis patients. Although he cured hundreds of cases successfully, many of his poorer patients became ill again when they returned to **crowded** and **unsanitary** living conditions at home. Dr. Bethune realized they could not be cured without **proper** living conditions and medical care. He wanted the medical system to provide the same level of health care for everyone. Dr. Bethune developed a plan for **socialized** medicine. Dr. Bethune and a group of **progressive** doctors presented their proposal for equal medical care for all to the government. However, they received a strong negative **reaction**. Dr. Bethune became unpopular among other doctors who thought his ideas were too **radical**.

At that time the Spanish Civil War was **raging** (1936-1939). A **spokesman** from the Committee to Aid Spanish Democracy visited Dr. Bethune. The Committee had chosen Dr. Bethune **to head** the Canadian Medical Unit in Madrid, Spain. At that time Dr. Bethune was one of the **top** paid doctors in Canada, 39 years old, and one of the world's top thoracic surgeons. That was a difficult decision. However, he left for Madrid on November 3, 1936.

While in Spain, Dr. Bethune did **pioneering** work with blood **transfusions**, developing the world's first **mobile** medical unit. This whole unit **contained dressings** for 500 **wounds**, and enough **supplies** and medicine for 100 operations. It could also be carried by just one **mule**. On many **occasions**, Dr. Bethune risked his life to deliver blood to the front line. Dr. Bethune returned to Canada on June 6, 1937 but he did not stay for a long time.

In 1938, Dr. Bethune went to China to help Mao Tse-tung and the Red Army fight the Japanese **invaders**. He became the Red Army's Medical Chief and trained thousands of Chinese as medics and doctors. He operated at a **prodigiou**s **rate**; once he operated on 115 patients in 69 hours without stopping even when under heavy **artillery** fire.

Unfortunately, Dr. Bethune soon lost his life while operating a Chinese soldier. Tales were told of this **extraordinary** Canadian who was **undaunted** by difficult conditions, who gave his clothes, his food, and even his own blood to the wounded. However, as he was operating on the wounded soldier, Dr. Bethune accidentally cut his finger because there were no **rubber** gloves. Very dangerous **bacteria** from the wounded soldier **penetrated** his blood. Although he **was aware of** the danger, he **refused** to take any medicine because he said," The soldiers need the medication more than I do." He died from blood **poisoning** at Huang Shiko, North China on November, 1939.

Many Canadian may have not heard about this famous international **humanitarian** Canadian. Recently, Dr. Bethune's **recognition** in Canada has resulted from his status as a hero in the People's Republic of China and the **impact** of this on Sino-Canadian relations. Throughout China, memorials have been **erected** **to** **extol** Bethune's example. The Model Hospital where he worked has been rebuilt. His **bomb** **shelter** in the side of a hill, the destroyed temple in which he operated, and houses in which he lived have all been **restored** as museums. All grade 3 children in China read Dr. Bethune's story in their reading books. In 1950, his body was moved to the Cemetery of Martyrs, which is **dedicated** to the more than 3.2 million Chinese soldiers who died in the war in Shijiazhuang. The world lost a great **unselfish**, international Canadian hero with Bethune's death on November 12, 1939.[6] Many statues of the extraordinary Canadian have been erected throughout China.[7]

Mao Tse-Tung and Dr. Norman Bethune   Dr. Bethune's tomb in China.

Practice Your Knowledge

Exercise #1—Vocabulary study

Task 1—Check the meaning of the following words in your dictionary. Copy the definitions.

---

[6] You can read more about Dr. Norman Bethune in a book written by Governor General of Canada, Adrianne Clarkson in her book "Extraordinary Canadians: Norman Bethune", published in 2009.

[7] More information can be found at http://www.pc.gc.ca/lhn-nhs/on/bethune/natcul/natcul1_e.asp

Task 2—Find the sentence with the same word from the text and copy it or write your own sentence. Follow the example with the word **"interrupt"**:

Definition—break an action off, cut an action short
Sentence—After her serious illness, Mrs. Green interrupted her studies.

➢ enlisted
Definition . . . .
. . . .
Sentence . . . .
. . . .

➢ stretcher bearer
Definition . . . .
. . . .
Sentence . . . .
. . . .

➢ demand
Definition . . . .
. . . .
Sentence . . . .
. . . .

➢ inevitable
Definition . . . .
. . . .
Sentence . . . .
. . . .

➢ frequently
Definition . . . .
. . . .
Sentence . . . .
. . . .

➢ remain
Definition . . . .
. . . .
Sentence . . . .
. . . .

➢ controversial
Definition . . . .
. . . .
Sentence . . . .
. . . .

➢ permanently
Definition . . . .
. . . .
Sentence . . . .
. . . .

➢ compression
Definition . . . .
. . . .
Sentence . . . .
. . . .

➢ artificial
Definition . . . .
. . . .
Sentence . . . .
. . . .

➢ surgery
Definition . . . .
. . . .
Sentence . . . .
. . . .

➢ surgeon
Definition . . . .
. . . .
Sentence . . . .
. . . .

➢ tuberculosis (TBC)
Definition . . . .
. . . .
Sentence . . . .
. . . .

➢ unsanitary
Definition . . . .
. . . .
Sentence . . . .
. . . .
➢ socialized
Definition . . . .
. . . .
Sentence . . . .
. . . .
➢ proper
Definition . . . .
. . . .
Sentence . . . .
. . . .
➢ spokesman
Definition . . . .
. . . .
Sentence . . . .
. . . .
➢ radical
Definition . . . .
. . . .
Sentence . . . .
. . . .
➢ to head
Definition . . . .
. . . .
Sentence . . . .
. . . .
➢ top paid
Definition . . . .
. . . .
Sentence . . . .
. . . .

➢ pioneering
Definition . . . .
. . . .
Sentence . . . .
. . . .
➢ transfusion
Definition . . . .
. . . .
Sentence . . . .
. . . .
➢ mobile
Definition . . . .
. . . .
Sentence . . . .
. . . .
➢ contain
Definition . . . .
. . . .
Sentence . . . .
. . . .
➢ dressing
Definition . . . .
. . . .
Sentence . . . .
. . . .
➢ supplies
Definition . . . .
. . . .
Sentence . . . .
. . . .
➢ mule
Definition . . . .
. . . .
Sentence . . . .
. . . .

➢ blood poisoning
Definition . . . .
. . . .
Sentence . . . .
. . . .
➢ impact
Definition . . . .
. . . .
Sentence . . . .
. . . .
➢ unselfish
Definition . . . .
. . . .
Sentence . . . .
. . . .
➢ attend
Definition . . . .
. . . .
Sentence . . . .
. . . .
➢ lumber
Definition . . . .
. . . .
Sentence . . . .
. . . .
➢ divorce
Definition . . . .
. . . .
Sentence . . . .
. . . .
➢ to waste
Definition . . . .
. . . .
Sentence . . . .
. . . .

➢ treatment

Definition . . . .
. . . .

Sentence . . . .
. . . .

➢ collapse

Definition . . . .
. . . .

Sentence . . . .
. . . .

➢ recover

Definition . . . .
. . . .

Sentence . . . .
. . . .

➢ crowded

Definition . . . .
. . . .

Sentence . . . .
. . . .

➢ progressive

Definition . . . .
. . . .

Sentence . . . .
. . . .

➢ reaction

Definition . . . .
. . . .

Sentence . . . .
. . . .

➢ raging

Definition . . . .
. . . .

Sentence . . . .
. . . .

➢ wound
Definition . . . .
. . . .
Sentence . . . .
. . . .
➢ prodigious
Definition . . . .
. . . .
Sentence . . . .
. . . .
➢ rate
Definition . . . .
. . . .
Sentence . . . .
. . . .
➢ artillery
Definition . . . .
. . . .
Sentence . . . .
. . . .
➢ undaunted
Definition . . . .
. . . .
Sentence . . . .
. . . .
➢ rubber
Definition . . . .
. . . .
Sentence . . . .
. . . .
➢ bacteria
Definition . . . .
. . . .
Sentence . . . .
. . . .

➤ penetrate

Definition . . . .

. . . .

Sentence . . . .

. . . .

➤ refuse

Definition . . . .

. . . .

Sentence . . . .

. . . .

➤ humanitarian

Definition . . . .

. . . .

Sentence . . . .

. . . .

Exercise #2: VOCABULARY BUILDING—Insert the right word from the list in the blanks. The sentences are taken from the text "Unknown in Canada, Famous in the World". Make the necessary changes to the words.

enlisted	inevitable	surgery	surgeon
determined	controversial	demand	realize
temporarily	unsanitary	radical	mobile
pioneering	dressing	occasion	medics
impact	status		

1. Then again his education was interrupted when he _____ as a stretcher bearer in World War I.
2. He became the Red Army's Medical Chief and trained thousands of Chinese as _____ and doctors.
3. On many _____, Dr. Bethune risked his life to deliver blood to the front line.
4. Only recently, Dr. Bethune's recognition in Canada has resulted from his _____ as a hero in the People's Republic of China and the _____ of this on Sino-Canadian relations.

5. The artificial pneumothorax is an insertion of air into the chest so as to collapse one lung either permanently or _____ depending on the case to let the other lung recover.
6. Dr. Bethune _____ they could not be cured without proper living conditions and medical care.
7. His wife, Frances, was _____ to stay by his side.
8. Although he cured hundreds of cases successfully, many of his poorer patients became ill again when they returned to crowded and _____ living conditions at home.
9. Dr. Bethune became unpopular among other doctors who thought his ideas were too _____.
10. This whole unit contained _____ for 500 wounds, and enough supplies and medicine for 100 operations.
11. Bethune _____ a divorce and sent Frances back to Scotland.
12. Dr. Bethune left New York for Montreal to study thoracic _____ under Dr. Archibald.
13. While in Spain, Dr. Bethune did _____ work with blood transfusions, developing the world's first _____ medical unit.
14. While at Trudeau Sanatorium, Bethune read about a new and _____ treatment for tuberculosis called compression therapy.
15. Bethune had accepted his _____ death.
16. From 1928 to 1936, Dr. Bethune worked as a thoracic _____ in Montreal.

Exercise #3: VOCABULARY BUILDING—New words used in a new context. Insert the right word from the list in the blanks. The sentences are not taken from the text but the words are used in the same meaning. Work with a friend:

controversial	demand	determined	mobile
temporarily	unsanitary	radical	medics
status	inevitable	occasion	surgeon
pioneering	dressing	realize	impact
surgery	enlisted		

1. Many young men and women are _____ in the army.
2. She underwent a very risky _____.
3. The difficult weather conditions had a negative _____ in the morning commute in the small town.
4. He used his diplomatic _____ to escape arrest.
5. The victory of people fighting for their freedom is _____.
6. Same sex marriage issues have become a _____ point of discussion.
7. On the _____ of Queen's visit, a new road was named after her.
8. He dreams to one day become a _____ and save many lives.
9. The study of academic English _____ many hours of work daily.
10. A group of doctors have built a _____ service to offer vaccines in neighborhoods.
11. Take this pill because it will _____ help with the pain but you must see your doctor tomorrow for a more permanent cure.
12. If you call 911, the _____ will rush to give the first medical assistance.
13. She needs to go to the hospital to change the _____ on her wound.
14. This _____ way of building cars will reduce the air pollution.
15. People are not following the leader because they think that her ideas are too _____.
16. Finally, he _____ that learning academic English does not happen by magic overnight.

Exercise #4: VOCABULARY BUILDING—Match the words below with the definitions in the box.

1. . . . . . . **status**   a) dirty, not clean, unhealthy
2. . . . . . . **determined**   b) for the moment, briefly, for a short time
3. . . . . . . **inevitable**   c) movable, portable, transportable
4. . . . . . . **occasion**   d) require, ask for, claim
5. . . . . . . **surgeon**   e) hot topic, notorious issue
6. . . . . . . **controversial**   f) medical doctor who performs operations

7. ...... **demand**   g) expected, certain, bound to happen
8. ...... **mobile**   h) strong-minded, firm, single-minded
9. ...... **radical**   i) ground-breaking, revolutionary, new
10. ...... **pioneering**   j) bandage, covering
11. ...... **dressing**   k) understand, recognize, comprehend
12. ...... **realize**   l) surgical procedure, operation
13. ...... **impact**   m) influence, effect,
14. ...... **surgery**   n) joined, enrolled, signed up, recruit
15. ...... **enlisted**   o) fundamental, major, extremist
16. ...... **temporarily**   p) rank, position, category, importance
17. ...... **unsanitary**   q) event, occurrence, circumstance

Exercise #5—Anagrams. Unscramble the words and write sentences:

- ctpami_____ ....
....
....
- gnsisder_____ ....
....
- laradic_____ ....
....
- cacosnoi_____ ....
....
- tsatsu_____ ....
....
- ortocnrevlias_____ ....
....
- tayrnasnui_____ ....
....
....

- egyrrsu_____ . . . .
. . . .
. . . .
- deentsil_____ . . . .
. . . .
. . . .

Exercise #6: Answer the following Wh-questions about the story:

1. Where was Norman Bethune born? . . . .
. . . .
2. Where did he study? . . . .
. . . .
3. When did he get sick? . . . .
. . . .
4. What was he diagnosed with? . . . .
. . . .
5. When did he go to Spain? . . . .
. . . .
6. Was he a famous doctor? Why? . . . .
. . . .
7. Where did he go after he returned from Spain? . . . .
. . . .
8. What made Dr. Bethune unpopular among his colleagues in Canada?
. . . .
. . . .
9. What made him famous in China? . . . .
. . . .
10. How does Dr. Bethune's legacy inspire you? . . . .
. . . .
. . . .

Exercise #7: Write 2-3 paragraphs about Dr. Bethune's life and how it inspired many people, including you. Describe his life and his contributions to the international community. Also, talk about the lessons you learned from the life of this doctor without borders.

Literature Focus: Personal Response

Writing a Personal Response to a story is a great responsibility. When you are looking for new and unique ways to express your feelings about a story or a novel you have read. It is good to include relevant information regarding the story's or novel's literary elements, as well as your opinions and reactions. Writing a Personal Response is a way of reflecting on a story and expressing your reaction to the reading. There are some rules related to writing a Personal Response and you must be as creative as possible, tapping into areas beyond what you learn in Language Arts. There are different ways of writing a personal response to a reading. You may choose any of the following ideas for writing a personal response.

- Write a letter to one of the characters in the story, novel. Ask him/her questions as well as tell him/her about yourself.
- Which character is most like you? Why?
- If the main characters from two different stories or novels could actually meet, who would you want to meet with whom? Why? What would their meeting be like?
- Move the setting of the story by changing the time and the place. What would the story be like now?
- Why did the author write this particular story? Express your opinion.
- Pretend you are a journalist whose job is to interview one of the characters. Write your interview.
- You have become a character in one of the stories. Describe your experience during a conflict.
- Write a poem about one of the stories. Touch on the characters, setting, plot, and theme.
- Rewrite a portion of the story as a dialogue or a play.
- Create a mini story wheel for your story, novel.

- Create a story timeline for your story that consists of at least ten links.
- Compare and contrast one of your stories with another that you have read for class this year or last. Remember to include how the stories are alike and how they are different.
- Redesign the front and back cover of your story. Include the pertinent information as well as a blurb on the back.

This is only the beginning of ideas! Be creative. You'll be pleasantly surprised by what you can accomplish.

Homework: Write your personal response to one of the stories you studied in the theme Special People, Special Deeds: Town Hero, Vote of Confidence, Marathon of Hope, or A Doctor Without Borders. Choose some items from the Literature Focus to lead you into writing your personal response.

<u>Exercise</u> #8—Prepare a Power Point presentation for the story "Unknown in Canada, Famous in the World" " or "China's Beloved Hero". Your power point must consist of a cover slide and 5 content slides. The content in the slides must be concise and you must use font Times Roman size 14. Use slide transition and animation of your choice in your presentation. Prepare to present the Power Point in class. Use the new words you learned in this unit in your presentation and underline them in the slides.

Supplemental reading: REQUIRED—Carefully read the following information about Dr. Bethune and write your personal response in your reading log.

China's Beloved Hero

One of China's great heroes isn't Chinese at all—he's an extraordinary Canadian! Norman Bethune was born in Gravenhurst, Ontario in 1890, a long way from northwestern China where he died from blood poisoning in 1939. After working as a stretcher bearer in the First World War until he was wounded at Ypres, France, Norman continued his medical studies at the University of Toronto. He then re-enlisted as a surgeon in the British navy, spending the last six months of the war as a medical officer with Canadian airmen in France. This was just the beginning of a long list of contributions that Dr. Bethune made to helping mankind. Besides many other deeds, he set up a free medical clinic for the poor in Montréal. He invented and refined many surgical instruments, some of which are still in use today.

During the Spanish Civil War in 1936, Dr. Bethune pioneered mobile blood transfusion services to bring donated blood to those wounded in battle. Bethune left for China in 1938, when he learned that there were not enough trained doctors to take care of the people wounded in the war with Japan. Dr. Bethune began to train individuals in first aid, sanitary practices and simple surgical procedures. He established teaching and nursing hospitals, developed mobile medical services and led mobile units through the mountains on horseback. In October 1939, while operating without surgical gloves on a wounded Chinese soldier, Dr. Bethune accidentally cut his hand. He developed an infection that, without the needed penicillin, developed into blood poisoning. He died on November 12, 1939.

Mao Zedong, leader of the People's Republic of China from 1949 to 1976, wrote a tribute to Norman Bethune, an essay that all Chinese schoolchildren are required to read even today. There is a statue, pavilion, museum, school and hospital dedicated to him in China.

Norman Bethune in front of a Canadian
Blood Transfusion Unit

Watercolour self-portrait of Norman Bethune
lying sick in bed

Dr. Norman Bethune, Gravenhurst, Ontario, 1920 [8]

STUDY TIP—As your English proficiency improves, start reading novels, but read for the story, not vocabulary. Read a chapter, then if you see repetitive vocabulary, look it up and then read again. As you advance through the novel, you will forget about vocabulary and start enjoying the story.

SPOT THE MISTAKE—Find the mistakes and fix them. Write the correct sentence:

This lady .... is reading a novel . . . .
. . . .
. . . .
. . . .
. . . .
. . . .

REMEMBER THIS—The adverbs **often, usually, sometimes** and **occasionally** can a) go at the beginning of a sentence, e.x.: **Sometimes** I go swimming. **Often** we surf the internet. b) Sometimes these adverbs are put at **the end of the sentence**. We read books **occasionally.**

---

[8]   http://www.collectionscanada.gc.ca/obj/002027/f1/a124375-v6.jpg

DID YOU KNOW?—You burn more calories eating celery than the calories it contains. The more celery you eat, the thinner you become.

LANGUAGE BANK—In this lesson you learned:

Active words	Recycled words	Passive words
1. attend	1. country	1. relevant
2. interrupt	2. anybody	2. specialist
3. lumber	3. medical	3. commitment
4. enlist	4. patient	4. responsibility
5. tuberculosis (TBC)	5. service	5. look or
6. demand	6. determined	6. unique
7. divorce	7. accept	7. express
8. inevitable	8. lung	8. regarding
9. waste	9. temorarely	9. opinion
10. frequently	10. cure	10. relate to . . . .
11. contraversial	11. patient	11. possible
12. treatment	12. conditions	12. tap into
13. artificial	13. medicine	13. pretend
14. collapse	14. equal	14. conflict
15. pernanently	15. government	15. dialogue
16. recover	16. however	16. pertinent
17. surgery	17. receive	17. airmen
18. surgeon	18. (un)popular	18. contribution
19. crowded	19. difficult	19. mankind
20. unsanitary	20. decision	20. invent
21. proper	21. blood	21. refine
22. socialized	22. become	22. infection
23. progressive	23. unfortunately	23. tribute
24. reaction	24. dangerous	24. essay

25. radical
26. ranging
27. spokesman
28. to head
29. top paid
30. pioneering
31. transfusion
32. wound
33. mobile
34. contain
35. dressing
36. supplies
37. mule
38. occasion
39. invador
40. prodigious
41. rate
42. artillery
43. extraordinary
44. undaunted
45. rubber
46. bacteria
47. penetrate
48. refuse
49. poisening
50. humanitarian
51. recognition
52. impact
53. erect
54. extol
55. restore
56. dedicate
57. unselfish
58. remain

25. medication
26. throughout
27. destroyed
28. include
29. information
30. creative
31. particular
32. journalist
33. deed

Expressions: set up, stretcher bearer, give up on himself, bomb shelter, compression therapy, was aware of

Lesson #5—The Braille Alphabet

⠃⠑ ⠅⠊⠝⠙ ⠞⠕ ⠕⠞⠓⠑⠗⠎

Be   kind   to   others

Learning Goals: A—Learn how to be courageous
B—Improve English proficiency
C—Learn to write a topic sentence

Language Focus—Topic sentence

Before you read, look at the picture and answer these questions:

1. What kind of alphabet do you use in your first language? . . . .
. . . .
. . . .

2. Was it difficult for you to learn the English alphabet? . . . .
. . . .
. . . .
. . . .

3. How many kinds of alphabets are there in the world? . . . .
. . . .
. . . .

4. Do you know anybody with disabilities who has succeeded in life? . . . .
. . . .
. . . .

5. How do the blind people learn how to read and write? . . . .
. . . .
. . . .
. . . .

THE BLIND WRITER

(In our **encounters** with EAL students we will learn a lot of new and **interesting** things. Let's start by listening to their discussion about the man who **invented** the Braille alphabet, the alphabet for the **blind**. Mr. Knowitall enters the classroom. He has been sick with the **flu** for a few days. Nick has led class discussions while Mr. Knowitall was sick. Mr. Knowitall is still not feeling well; he **coughs** as he enters the classroom.)

Mr. Knowitall: Good morning everyone. It is so good to be back with you and out of bed. I really **missed** you. How did it go yesterday Nick?

Nick: Of course, it was not the same as when you teach the class, Mr. Knowitall, but we **managed**. Everybody **contributed** to a **normal** and enjoyable class.

Karen: In fact, Nick was a very good teacher, Mr. Knowitall. (Andrew turns to her angrily with a **jealous** look for **complementing** Nick)

Nisa: Yes, Nick did a very good job yesterday, (sees Andrew's reaction to their **comments**, turns to Andrew), didn't he Andrew?

Andrew: (reluctantly) I **guess** so. (Changes the subject) How are you feeling today Mr. Knowitall?

Mr. Knowitall: (understands that something is not right with Andrew or that he may be jealous of Nick becoming popular with the girls, especially Karen) I am doing fine, thanks. It is nice to hear that the class went well in my **absence**. Even though I stayed in bed yesterday, my throat is still very **sore**. I wish there was a special way for me to **avoid** talking today.

Nick :(makes a **suggestion**) We could be creative and use a special way to **communicate.**

Andrew: (trying to **outwit** Nick) Let us use the Braille alphabet to communicate.

Mr. Knowitall: (smiles) That would not help my throat much, would it Andrew? (Andrew **blushes**). Braille alphabet does not help people who have problems with their throats but with their eyes.

Nick: (**genuinely** interested) What is the Braille alphabet and who uses it, Andrew?

Andrew: (looks at Karen, happy that he knows something that others, especially Nick, do not know) Braille is a system of **embossed typed** letters used by blind and **partially sighted** people for reading and writing. It has been **adapted** into almost every known language. It is used everywhere from bus stops and maps to music **notations**, **elevators**, and books for the blind.

Nisa: Thanks, Andrew. I have never heard of it. Can we talk about the Braille alphabet today, Mr. Knowitall? Andrew can lead our discussion as he knows about it.

Andrew: I would be happy to do that on condition that everyone will contribute to the class by reading a part of the information I have **gathered**. That will help us learn more and it will help Mr. Knowitall with his throat.

All students: We agree to that.

Mr. Knowitall: Here is what we will do: Andrew has prepared **index cards** with different **paragraphs** that will tell the history of the Braille alphabet. He will give each one of you a paragraph to read first, **check** the words that you do not know in the **dictionary** and then **explain** the information in your paragraph to the group. Andrew, please give everybody one of these paragraphs. (Andrew **proudly** distributes the paragraphs) I will start with the first paragraph and then you will follow with your readings in the order of the numbers you have on the index cards.

Nick: What do we do if there are words that we do not know in the paragraph we read, Mr. Knowitall?

Mr. Knowitall: First, you try to **figure out** the pronunciation, if you can't, I will help. Then try to guess the meaning of the word from the sentence, if you can't, look for the definition in the dictionary. After we finish reading, we will discuss the new words. Here we go: (Starts reading) Louis Braille was born in 1809 and died in 1852. He was the 12-year-old French boy, who was blind and invented the alphabet that changed the world of reading and writing, **forever**. Louis was from a small town called Coupvray, near Paris. Louis became blind due to an accident, when he was 3 years old. One day he was in his dad's **harness workshop**. Louis tried to be like his dad, but something **went very wrong**; he **grabbed** a **sharp tool** for making **holes**, and the tool **slid** and hurt his eye. The wound was infected, and the infection **spread**. Soon, Louis was blind in both eyes.

Nisa: It is so sad to **lose** both your eyes at such a young age. It is my turn now. (reads) **All of a sudden**, Louis needed a new way to learn. He stayed at his old school for two more years, but he couldn't learn everything just by listening. **Things were looking up** when Louis received a **scholarship** to the Royal Institution for Blind Youth in Paris, when he was ten. However, even there, most of the teachers just talked to the students. The **library** had fourteen **huge** books with raised letters that were very hard to carry or to read. Louis was **impatient**.

Andrew: I will read paragraph #3. Here I go. (reads) In 1821, a **former** soldier, named Charles Barbier, visited Louis' school. Barbier shared his invention called "night writing," a **code** of twelve raised **dots** that let soldiers share **top-secret** information on the battlefield without even having to speak. Although, the code was too difficult for the soldiers, it was not so difficult at all for the twelve year old Louis!

Nick: I have paragraph #4. (reads) Louis **trimmed** Barbier's twelve dots into only six dots for his alphabet when he was twelve years old. He **ironed out** the whole new system by the time he was fifteen, then **published** the first-ever Braille book in 1829. He was only twenty years old. But did he stop there? No way! In 1837, he added symbols for math and music to the Braille writing. But since the public was **sceptical** about the Braille alphabet, blind students had to study Braille **on their own**. Even at the Royal Institution, where Louis taught after he **graduated**, Braille wasn't taught until after his death. Braille began to spread **worldwide** in 1868, when a group of British men, known as the Royal National Institute for the Blind, **took up the cause.**

Karen: I think I have the last paragraph. (reads) Today **practically** every country in the world uses Braille. Braille books have double-sided pages, which saves a lot of space. Braille signs help blind people **get around** in public spaces. And, most important, blind people can communicate **independently**, without needing print. Louis **proved** that if you are motivated, you could do **incredible** things.

Andrew: So, how does the Braille alphabet work, Mr. Knowitall?

Mr. Knowitall: All it takes is six dots and six **bumps** in different **patterns**, like star **constellations,** spreading out over the page. They form numbers, letters, and words. Who made this code? A twelve year old boy, much younger than you.

Andrew: (**amazed** by this extraordinary boy) This is incredible. (speaking to himself) And I have both eyes, lots of books, dictionaries, and computers and do not study! Braille has inspired me; I will never **skip** my homework or **complain** that there are too many new words to learn.

Nick: (laughs) If I know you Andrew, you will soon forget about this inspiring lesson.

Andrew: No man, this is incredible. Just wait and see me.

Mr. Knowitall: You will have the chance to show us that you can keep your promises Andrew. Soon we will start learning how to write good paragraphs in English. It takes a lot of learning and practice **to master** paragraph writing. I know you all can do it. Thanks for a great class today everybody. Remember to work with the new words from our reading about Louis Braille and write a sentence for each new word. See you tomorrow.

Practice Your Knowledge

Exercise **#1**—Vocabulary study

Task 1—Check the meaning of the following words in your dictionary. Copy the definitions.

Task 2—Find the sentence with the same word from the text and copy it or write your own sentence. Follow the example with the word **"manage"**:

   Definition—survive; continue despite difficulties or lack of resources
   Sentence—I <u>managed</u> to find my way to the new library without a map.

➢ contribute
Definition . . . .
. . . .
Sentence . . . .
. . . .

➢ encounter
Definition . . . .
. . . .
Sentence . . . .
. . . .

➢ invent
Definition . . . .
. . . .
Sentence . . . .
. . . .

➢ normal
Definition . . . .
. . . .
Sentence . . . .
. . . .

➢ introduce

Definition . . . .
. . . .
Sentence . . . .
. . . .

➢ avoid

Definition . . . .
. . . .
Sentence . . . .
. . . .

➢ communicate

Definition . . . .
. . . .
Sentence . . . .
. . . .

➢ outwit

Definition . . . .
. . . .
Sentence . . . .
. . . .

➢ embossed (letters)

Definition . . . .
. . . .
Sentence . . . .
. . . .

➢ typed

Definition . . . .
. . . .
Sentence . . . .
. . . .

➢ interesting

Definition . . . .
. . . .
Sentence : . . . .
. . . .

➢ adapted

Definition . . . .
. . . .

Sentence . . . .
. . . .

➢ blind

Definition . . . .
. . . .

Sentence . . . .
. . . .

➢ flu

Definition . . . .
. . . .

Sentence . . . .
. . . .

➢ harness

Definition . . . .
. . . .

Sentence . . . .
. . . .

➢ slid

Definition . . . .
. . . .

Sentence . . . .
. . . .

➢ grab

Definition . . . .
. . . .

Sentence . . . .
. . . .

➢ cough

Definition . . . .
. . . .

Sentence . . . .
. . . .

➢ miss

Definition . . . .
. . . .
Sentence . . . .
. . . .

➢ scholarship

Definition . . . .
. . . .
Sentence . . . .
. . . .

➢ impatient

Definition . . . .
. . . .
Sentence . . . .
. . . .

➢ former

Definition . . . .
. . . .
Sentence . . . .
. . . .

➢ code

Definition . . . .
. . . .
Sentence . . . .
. . . .

➢ dot

Definition . . . .
. . . .
Sentence . . . .
. . . .

➢ manage

Definition . . . .
. . . .
Sentence . . . .
. . . .

➢ trim

Definition . . . .

. . . .

Sentence . . . .

. . . .

➢ jealous

Definition . . . .

. . . .

Sentence . . . .

. . . .

➢ publish

Definition . . . .

. . . .

Sentence . . . .

. . . .

➢ sceptical

Definition . . . .

. . . .

Sentence . . . .

. . . .

➢ on their own

Definition . . . .

. . . .

Sentence . . . .

. . . .

➢ worldwide

Definition . . . .

. . . .

Sentence . . . .

. . . .

➢ compliment

Definition . . . .

. . . .

Sentence . . . .

. . . .

➢ graduate
Definition . . . .
. . . .
Sentence . . . .
. . . .
➢ practically
Definition . . . .
. . . .
Sentence . . . .
. . . .
➢ incredible
Definition . . . .
. . . .
Sentence . . . .
. . . .
➢ bump
Definition . . . .
. . . .
Sentence . . . .
. . . .
➢ pattern
Definition . . . .
. . . .
Sentence . . . .
. . . .
➢ constellation
Definition . . . .
. . . .
Sentence . . . .
. . . .
➢ comment
Definition . . . .
. . . .
Sentence . . . .
. . . .

➤ complain
Definition . . . .
. . . .
Sentence . . . .
. . . .

➤ skip
Definition . . . .
. . . .
Sentence . . . .
. . . .

➤ guess
Definition . . . .
. . . .
Sentence . . . .
. . . .

➤ to master
Definition . . . .
. . . .
Sentence . . . .
. . . .

➤ absence
Definition . . . .
. . . .
Sentence . . . .
. . . .

➤ sore
Definition . . . .
. . . .
Sentence . . . .
. . . .

➤ suggestion
Definition . . . .
. . . .
Sentence . . . .
. . . .

➢ blush

Definition . . . .

. . . .

Sentence . . . .

. . . .

➢ genuinely

Definition . . . .

. . . .

Sentence . . . .

. . . .

➢ typed

Definition . . . .

. . . .

Sentence . . . .

. . . .

➢ notation

Definition . . . .

. . . .

Sentence . . . .

. . . .

➢ elevator

Definition . . . .

. . . .

Sentence . . . .

. . . .

➢ to gather

Definition . . . .

. . . .

Sentence . . . .

. . . .

➢ paragraph

Definition . . . .

. . . .

Sentence . . . .

. . . .

➢ to check

Definition . . . .

. . . .

Sentence . . . .

. . . .

➢ dictionary

Definition . . . .

. . . .

Sentence . . . .

. . . .

➢ explain

Definition . . . .

. . . .

Sentence . . . .

. . . .

➢ proudly

Definition . . . .

. . . .

Sentence . . . .

. . . .

➢ forever

Definition . . . .

. . . .

Sentence . . . .

. . . .

➢ sharp

Definition . . . .

. . . .

Sentence . . . .

. . . .

➢ tool

Definition . . . .

. . . .

Sentence . . . .

. . . .

➢ hole
Definition . . . .
. . . .
Sentence . . . .
. . . .
➢ spread
Definition . . . .
. . . .
Sentence . . . .
. . . .
➢ lose
Definition . . . .
. . . .
Sentence . . . .
. . . .
➢ library
Definition . . . .
. . . .
Sentence . . . .
. . . .
➢ huge
Definition . . . .
. . . .
Sentence . . . .
. . . .
➢ independently
Definition . . . .
. . . .
Sentence . . . .
. . . .
➢ prove
Definition . . . .
. . . .
Sentence . . . .
. . . .

➢ incredible

Definition . . . .
. . . .

Sentence . . . .
. . . .

Exercise #2: VOCABULARY BUILDING—Insert the right word from the list in the blanks. The sentences are taken from the text "The Braille Alphabet;" make the necessary changes to the words.

encounters	contribute	outwit	adapt	embossed
harness	grab	infect	scholarship	impatient
trim	skeptical	publish	motivated	constellation
amazed	master	skip	complain	bumps

1. I will never _____my homework or _____ that there are too many new words to learn.
2. It takes a lot of learning and practice _____ paragraph writing.
3. Andrew: (_____) This is incredible.
4. All it takes is six dots and six _____ in different patterns, like star _____, spreading out over the page.
5. Louis proved that if you are _____, you could do incredible things.
6. He ironed out the whole new system by the time he was fifteen, then _____ the first-ever Braille book in 1829.
7. But since the public was _____about the Braille alphabet, blind students had to study Braille on their own.
8. Louis _____Barbier's twelve dots into only six dots for his alphabet when he was twelve years old.
9. Louis was _____.
10. Things were looking up when Louis received a _____ to the Royal Institution for Blind Youth in Paris, when he was ten.
11. The wound was _____, and the infection spread.

12. Louis tried to be like his dad, but something went very wrong; he _____ a sharp tool for making holes, and the tool slid and hurt his eye.

13. One day he was in his dad's _____ workshop.

14. Braille is a system of _____ typed letters used by blind and partially sighted people for reading and writing.

15. It has been _____ into almost every known language.

16. Andrew: (trying to _____ Nick) Let us use the Braille alphabet to communicate.

17. Everybody _____ to a normal class.

18. In our _____ with him and his students we will learn a lot of new, interesting things.

Exercise #3: VOCABULARY BUILDING—New words used in a new context. Insert the right word from the list in the blanks. The sentences are not taken from the text but the words are used in the same meaning. Work with a friend:

embossed	harness	grab	infect	master
skip	complain	bumps	publish	motivated
constellation	amazed	encounters	contribute	outwit
adapt	scholarship	impatient	trim	skeptical

1. He was _____ about the results of the experiment.

2. Many teachers have _____ the new teaching method to improve their students' academic English.

3. The mother was _____ at her daughter's performance in the Christmas concert.

4. The city has put speed _____ on the roads of my neighborhood to protect the children from speeding cars.

5. The doctors decided to amputate the soldier's arm because it was badly _____.

6. The hairdresser _____ the boy's hair.

7. Our school's team in the math competition _____ the rival team through their answers.

8. In a summer night I want to look at the clear sky and find star _____.

9. The students are _____ because the teacher asked them to finish the homework for tomorrow.
10. John was late for school so, he _____ a sandwich and left.
11. Many ESL students are _____ to finish their ESL program and join the mainstream classes.
12. Dr. Bethune has_____ to world peace all his life without considering the borders or the countries where he served.
13. The teacher explained to his students that there are many _____ available for the students with high grades.
14. Terry Fox' example and bravery has _____ many people to join forces in raising money for cancer research.
15. The teacher asked Mike to bring his father to school to discuss the fact that Mike _____ many classes and may fail this class.
16. The Canadian soldiers have had many _____ with danger in their peacekeeping missions.
17. The young mother was trying to _____ her little boy's energies my enrolling him in many sport activities.
18. Dr. Speirs has _____ a number of articles in which she draws the reader's attention to issues related to equal rights for women.
19. It is not easy to _____ a foreign language while working and raising a family.
20. The name of the hero was _____ on his grave stone.

Exercise #34: VOCABULARY BUILDING—Match the words below with the definitions in the box.

1. ...... **trim**   a) stamp, decorate, make fancy, print
2. ...... **skeptical**   b) give shape, cut, clip
3. ...... **outwit**   c) disbelieving, doubtful, unconvinced
4. ...... **adapt**   d) annoyed, intolerant, eager, impulsive
5. ...... **scholarship**   e) group of stars, collection
6. ...... **constellation** f) outsmart, get the better of, the best
7. ...... **impatient**   g) become accustomed, adjust, modify
8. ...... **amazed**   h) money giving to a student to study
9. ...... **encounters**   i) become perfect in doing something

10. . . . . . . **contribute**   j) pass on a disease, a wound that gets worse
11. . . . . . . **motivate**   k) grasp, take hold of, seize
12. . . . . . . **publish**   l) protest about something, find fault with
13. . . . . . . **complain**   m) leave out, miss out, not attend
14. . . . . . . **skip**   n) make public, print out, distribute
15. . . . . . . **emboss**   o) inspire, encourage, cause to happen
16. . . . . . . **grab**   p) give contribution to, play a role in
17. . . . . . . **infect**   q) meeting, come across
18. . . . . . . **master**   r) shocked, surprised, astonished

Exercise #45—Anagrams—Unscramble the words below and write sentences:

- ontlalestcno_____ . . . .
. . . .
. . . .
- unetrsocne_____ . . . .
. . . .
. . . .
- ipsk_____ . . . .
. . . .
. . . .
- mpianocl_____ . . . .
. . . .
. . . .
- osbsem_____ . . . .
. . . .
. . . .
- eftcin_____ . . . .
. . . .
. . . .
- brag_____ . . . .
. . . .
. . . .
- ietnmiap_____ . . . .
. . . .
. . . .

- edzama_____ . . . .
. . . .
. . . .
- islhubp_____ . . . .
. . . .
. . . .
- tmri_____ . . . .
. . . .
. . . .

Exercise #5: Answer the following Wh-questions about the story:

1. How old was Louis Braille when he hurt his eyes? . . . .
. . . .
. . . .

2. What century did Louis Braille live? . . . .
. . . .
. . . .

3. When did things start to look up for Louis? . . . .
. . . .
. . . .

4. What was the difference between Barbier's alphabet and Braille's alphabet? . . . .
. . . .
. . . .

5. Why did the blind students study Braille alphabet on their own? . . . .
. . . .
. . . .

6. How old was Louis when he discovered the alphabet named after him? . . . .
. . . .
. . . .

7. How old was Louis when he died? . . . .
. . . .
. . . .

8. What did the British men from the Royal Institute do for the blind in 1868? . . . .
. . . .
. . . .

9. What was the significance of their actions at that time and now? . . . .
. . . .
. . . .
. . . .

10. What impressed you most from Louis Braille's life and achievements?
. . . .
. . . .
. . . .

Exercise #6:—Circle "T" if a sentence is true. Circle "N" if a sentence is not true. Circle "X" if you do not understand the sentence.
Example: T (This is **True**) **N** (This is **Not true**) **X** (I do **Not understand** the question)

- One person can lift this animal.   **T N X**
- Firefighters help put the blaze out.   **T N X**
- A family always has at least two people.   **T N X**
- You can go by road from London, England,   **T N X**
  to Toronto, Canada.

- This is a farm.   **T N X**
- Mothers express their concern for their   **T N X**
  children virtually every day.
- A society is made up of people living together.   **T N X**
- About 48 percent of the Canadian parliament   **T N X**
  members are women.
- It is important to get women perspectives   **T N X**
  into politics.
- He did his fair share to make the new   **T N X**
  discovery available.
- When something is ancient, it is very big.   **T N X**

- "To be determined" means to be happy. **T N X**
- My best friend was diagnosed with a new **T N X**
  and unknown disease.
- When something is impossible, it is easy to do it. **T N X**
- Terry Fox did a lot of research. **T N X**
- A square has five sides. **T N X**
- Boats are made to travel on land. **T N X**
- Cars cannot pass each other on a wide road. **T N X**
- When you look at something closely, **T N X**
  you can see the details.

- This part of the teapot is a handle. **T N X**

Exercise #7—Complete the words in bold.

- The dress you're wearing is **won**_____.
- It is the **ef**_____ that counts, not the thought.
- Children are **mo**_____ from the stories in this book.
- The **su**_____ was amputating the patients leg in the operating room.
- Laws are based on the principle of **de**_____.
- The mechanic had to replace the **st**_____ **wh**_____of the car.
- The doctor **di**_____ the patient with lung cancer.
- Mother Teresa was a great **hum**_____ who took care of poor people in the streets.
- This work is not up to your **usu**_____ standard.
- They were **sce**_____ about his project but still continued to support him.
- You must have been very brave to participate in such a **dan**_____ operation.
- The workers were repairing the **dera**_____ tracks of the train.
- The driver **swe**_____ the car to avoid the accident.
- Rocky Mountains are an **extr**_____ view in Canada.
- Immigrants were represented in the **parl**_____ by a remarkable journalist.

Grammar point—Paragraph writing—Topic sentence

What is a paragraph?—A paragraph is a number of sentences that are organized and coherent, and are all related to a single topic. Almost every piece of writing that is longer than a few sentences should be organized into paragraphs. This is because paragraphs show a reader where the ideas begin and end and help the reader see how ideas are organized and grasp its main points.

Paragraphs can contain many different kinds of information. A paragraph could contain a series of brief examples or a single long illustration of a general point. It might describe a place, character, or process; narrate a series of events; compare or contrast two or more things; classify items into categories; or describe causes and effects. Regardless of the kind of information they contain, all paragraphs share certain characteristics. One of the most important of these is a **topic sentence.**

TOPIC SENTENCE—A well-organized paragraph supports or develops a single controlling idea, which is expressed in a sentence called the topic sentence. A topic sentence has several important functions:

➢ it supports and explains what the paragraphs is about;
➢ it unifies the content of a paragraph and directs the order of the sentences;
➢ it advises the reader of the subject to be discussed and how the paragraph will discuss it.

Readers generally look to the first sentence in a paragraph to determine the subject and perspective of the paragraph. That is why it is often best to put the topic sentence at the very beginning of the paragraph. In some cases, however, it is more effective to place another sentence before the topic sentence—for example, a sentence linking the current paragraph to the previous one, or one that provides background information. The vast majority of paragraphs, however, should start with a topic sentence.

Here is an example of the way to arrange sentences in a paragraph:

a) Sentences in the following paragraph are not well organized, re-arrange them:

Garlic has been shown to reduce the risk of cardiovascular disease[9], and possess anti-microbial (Sivam, 2001) and antioxidant properties (Imai et al., 1994). This paragraph will explore research into garlic's potential roles in reducing cancer risk and in treating cancer. Garlic (Allium sativum L.) has been used for centuries for medicinal purposes. Its use for healing purposes can be traced back as far as 1550 B.C. when documentations of its therapeutic use first appear in Egypt (Hassan, 2003; Rivlin, 2001). In modern times, belief in the beneficial effects of garlic on health has led to it being used for a number of conditions.

Check your version against the following correct answer. Notice that the first sentence (in bold) is the topic sentence.

Garlic (Allium sativum L.) has been used for centuries for medicinal purposes. Its use for healing purposes can be traced back as far as 1550B.C. when documentations of its therapeutic use first appear in Egypt (Hassan, 2003; Rivlin, 2001). In modern times, belief in the beneficial effects of garlic on health has led to it being used for a number of conditions. Garlic has been shown to reduce the risk of cardiovascular disease (Aboul-Enein and Aboul-Enein, 2005), and possess anti-microbial (Sivam, 2001) and antioxidant properties (Imai et al., 1994). This essay will explore research into garlic's potential roles in reducing cancer risk and in treating cancer.

Exercise #6—Look at the following extract from an essay on a disease called "cystic fibrosis". Can you identify the topic sentence for this paragraph and complete the paragraph?

Cystic fibrosis (CF) is one of the most common genetic disorders. CF is inherited as an autosomal recessive trait and a defective gene causes the body to produce an abnormal amount of very thick, sticky mucus, which clogs the lungs and pancreas, interfering with breathing and digestion. This mucus builds up in the breathing passages in the lungs and the pancreas and respiratory complications develop from the blockage of the bronchial passages. Eventually, the cilia which are responsible for clearing the mucus are destroyed. In addition, the mucus traps bacteria which cause infections

---

[9]   (Aboul-Enein and Aboul-Enein, 2005)

and permanent damage to the lungs, and may block the ducts of the pancreas which contains enzymes necessary for the digestion of food.

sentence 1 _____

sentence 2 _____

sentence 3 _____

sentence 4 _____

sentence 5 _____

Homework:—Complete the following paragraph by creating a topic sentence that both identifies the particular character trait and creates enough interest to keep us reading. Re-arrange the order of the sentences if necessary. The possibilities, of course, are limitless.

Passage Title: A Love of Reading

Create a topic sentence . . . .
. . . .
. . . .
. . . .

When I was a young girl, I would make a tent out of my blankets and read mystery books late into the night. I still read cereal boxes at the breakfast table, newspapers while I am waiting at the dentist's, and gossip magazines while waiting in line at the grocery store. In fact, I'm a very talented reader. For example, I've mastered the art of talking on the phone while simultaneously reading my e-mails. But *what* I read doesn't matter all that much. In a pinch, I'll read junk mail, an old warranty, a furniture tag, or even, if I'm extremely desperate, a chapter or two in a textbook.

Supplemental reading: REQUIRED—Carefully read the following information about Louis Braille and write a personal response in your reading log.

It took a blind man to lead the way in creating a system that allows the blind to read. Louis Braille, a normal, healthy, French child at birth, became sightless when he was only three. At ten, he was placed in a home for the blind, a special state institution. But young Louis had great talent. He became a skilled musician. Soon he was appointed a church organist in Paris. When he was twenty-five, he became a teacher of the blind. To help his students with their studies, he worked hard to develop a special alphabet of raised indentations on thick paper so that his young students could study both written and musical works. This became known as the Braille system, which is used by the blind all over the world today.

As an eleven-year-old boy, Louis took a secret code devised for the military and saw in it the basis for written communication for blind individuals. Louis Braille enrolled at the National Institute of the Blind in Paris and spent nine years developing and refining the system of raised dots that has come to be known by his name—Braille Alphabet. The original military code was called "night writing" and was used by soldiers to communicate after dark. It was based on a twelve-dot cell, two dots wide by six dots high. Each dot or combination of dots within the cell stood for a letter or a phonetic sound. The problem with the military code was that the human fingertip could not feel all the dots with one touch. So, Louis Braille created a reading method based on a cell of six dots instead of twelve. This crucial improvement meant that a fingertip could encompass the entire cell unit with one touch and move rapidly from one cell to the next.

The system of embossed writing invented by Louis Braille gradually came to be accepted throughout the world as the fundamental form of written communication for blind individuals, and it remains today as he invented it in 1829. Over time, there has been some modification of the Braille system, particularly the addition of contractions representing groups of letters or whole words that appear frequently in a language. The use of contractions permits faster Braille reading and helps reduce the size of Braille books, making easier to use.

Several groups have been established over the last decades to modify and standardize the Braille code. A major goal is to develop easily understood contractions without making the code too complex. People who are totally blind are able to interact with the computer using assistive technologies today. In order to overcome their difficulties in reading, they mostly use screen reader software and Braille displays. A screen reader system speaks all the information which comes on the screen as well as the text which is typed on the keyboard in a human voice. Another method is using the Braille display, which makes the same information appear on a Braille line which blind people can read with their fingers. However, we cannot forget the young French blind man who invented the Braille alphabet when he was only twenty years old.

Exercise #7: Write 2-3 paragraphs about Louis Braille's life and how it inspired many people, including you. Make sure each of your paragraphs consists of:

a) Topic sentence (with a controlling idea)
b) body (supporting sentences—fact, example, reason, quote, data)
c) conclusion

Exercise #8-Create a power point presentation based on what you learned about Louis Braille. The following are some ideas you may consider:

❖ Who was Louis Braille?
❖ What happened to him?
❖ What did he achieve in his life?
❖ How does Braille's life inspire you?

STUDY TIP—The "SQ3R method" is a proven way to sharpen study skills. **SQ3R** stands for Survey, Question, Read, Recite, and Review. Take a moment now and write SQ3R down. It is a good slogan to commit to memory to carry out an effective study strategy.

SPOT THE MISTAKE—Find the mistakes and fix them. Write the correct sentence:

l o u i s

b r a i l l e

The picture shows that it is easy for a child play soccer . . . .
. . . .
. . . .
. . . .
. . . .
. . . .

REMEMBER THIS: How to use "who", "which", and "that"— Who refers to people. That and which refer to groups or things. That introduces essential information while which introduces nonessential information.

DID YOU KNOW?—The English word for a group of owls is "a parliament".

LANGUAGE BANK—In this lesson you learned:

Active words	Recycled words	Passive words
1. introduce	1. discussion	1. coherent
2. encounter	2. enter	2. related

3. interesting
4. invent
5. blind
6. flu
7. cough
8. miss
9. manage
10. contribute
11. normal
12. jealous
13. complement
14. comment
15. guess
16. absence
17. sore
18. avoid
19. suggestion
20. communicate
21. outfit
22. blush
23. genuinely
24. embossed
25. typed
26. adapt
27. notation
28. elevator
29. gather
30. paragraph
31. check
32. dictionary
33. explain
34. proudly
35. forever
36. harness
37. workshop
38. grab
39. sharp
40. tool
41. hole

3. sick
4. feeling
5. enjoyable
6. reaction
7. reluctantly
8. popular
9. become
10. especially
11. throat
12. special
13. creative
14. interested
15. letters
16. everyone
17. information
18. different
19. everybody
20. distribute
21. pronunciation
22. sentence
23. definition
24. due to
25. hurt
26. wound
27. infect
28. infection
29. share
30. raise
31. although
32. difficult
33. battlefield
34. amazed
35. extraordinary
36. inspire
37. contain
38. example
39. event
40. compare
41. effect

3. grasp
4. general
5. illustration
6. describe
7. brief
8. narrate
9. contrast
10. classify
11. cause
12. regardless
13. support
14. . unify
15. determine
16. perspective
17. effective
18. current
19. previous
20. majority
21. common
22. genetic
23. disorder
24. gene
25. abnormal
26. mucus
27. clog
28. respiratory
29. complication
30. blockage
31. bronchial
32. passage
33. permanent
34. trap
35. duct
36. enzyme
37. digestion
38. tent
39. blanket
40. gossip
41. warranty

42. to slide
43. spread
44. lose
45. scholarship
46. library
47. huge
48. impatient
49. former
50. code
51. dot
52. bump
53. trim
54. publish
55. sceptical
56. graduate
57. worldwide
58. practically
59. prove
60. pattern
61. skip
62. independently
63. incredible
64. constellation
65. complain

42. characteristics
43. important
44. thick
45. lung
46. responsible
47. destroy
48. bacteria
49. master

Expressions: partially sighted, index card, figure out, top-secret went(go) very wrong, all of a sudden, things were looking up iron put, on their own, took(take) up the cause, get around

Let us review our knowledge

Task #1—Review the vocabulary you learned in this book.

Active words   **Recycled words**   **Passive words**

THEME #1—LANGUAGE STRUCTURE

Lesson #1—An Extraordinary Painter (Plural of Nouns)

Active words	Recycled words	Passive words
1. welcome	1. proficiency	1. continue
2. intermediate	2. develop	2. perform
3. level(s)	3. excited	3. academic
4. subject(s)	4. glad	4. prefix(es)
5. unusual	5. dialogue(s)	5. suffix(es)
6. artistic	6. definition(s)	6. syllable(s)
7. famous	7. enjoy	7. root(s)
8. to analyze	8. vocabulary(ies)	8. to place
9. world(s)	9. agree	9. itself
10. practice	10. sentence(s)	10. kangaroo
11. painter(s)	11. important	11. rat(s)
12. software	12. need	12. jump
13. to paint	13. knowledge	13. leap
14. the paint	14. story(ies)	14. powerful
15. puzzled	15. totally	15. hind
16. impossible	16. fabulous	16. tail(s)
17. information	17. proud of	17. search
18. create(ed)	18. because	18. food
19. surprise(d)	19. unique	19. large
20. zoo(s)	20. excited	20. silky
21. zookeeper(s)	21. fur	
22. elephant	22. stuff	
23. happen	23. pouch(es)	
24. jar(s)	24. combine	

25. easel
26. piece
27. paper
28. point to . . . .
29. trunk
30. to dip
31. brush
32. to curl
33. the handle
34. to own
35. amazing
36. sharing
37. guy(s)
38. to master

25. oxygen
26. breathe
27. desert

Expressions: am(to be) sure, can hardly wait, are going to (do) . . . ,artistic skills

Lesson #2—Our Pets (Possessive Case)

1. neighborhood
2. walk
3. today
4. decide
5. about
6. pet(s)
7. way(s)
8. care
9. around
10. smile(s)
11. face(s)
12. great
13. hope
14. sunny
15. too
16. lazy
17. early
18. change
19. better
20. lifestyle(s)
21. store(s)
22. problem(s)
23. plan(s)

1. city
2. beautiful
3. usual
4. think
5. interesting
6. discussion
7. different
8. enter
9. enjoy
10. run
11. need
12. because
13. healthy
14. exercise
15. difficult
16. afternoon
17. cat
18. bird
19. share
20. sentence
21. wagon
22. handle
23. own

1. inflate
2. inflatable
3. common
4. along
5. tropical
6. waters
7. ordinary
8. appears
9. sticking out
10. disturb
11. stomach
12. air
13. belly
14. float
15. upward
16. surface
17. danger
18. pass
19. blow
20. twice
21. normal
22. confuse
23. actually

24. topic(s)
25. choose
26. prepare
27. pick
28. sidewalk(s)
29. wheel(s)
30. cut
31. nail(s)
32. often
33. become
34. start
35. bark
36. pass
37. bother
38. concern
39. safely
40. promise
41. excellent

24. yarn
25. sometimes
26. main
27. characteristic
28. pronunciation
29. easy
30. understand
31. protect
32. injure

Expressions: wake up, litter of kittens, pick up, take care, bring up

24. odd-looking
25. essay
26. organic
27. complain

Lesson #3—Mermaids (Personal Pronouns)

1. supplemental
2. continue
3. legend(s)
4. related to
5. compare
6. contrast
7. folks
8. the same
9. mermaids
10. ocean
11. handsome
12. similarities
13. differences
14. to sound
15. called
16. never
17. theme
18. however
19. intrigued

1. about
2. hope
3. topic
4. prepare
5. start
6. excellent
7. concern
8. contain
9. share
10. important
11. discuss
12. interesting
13. enjoy
14. decide
15. talking
16. thinking
17. inflatable
18. too
19. sometimes

1. wedding(s)
2. party(ies)
3. bride(s)
4. groom(s)
5. mountain(s)
6. drive
7. complain
8. beach(es)
9. postage
10. stamp(s)
11. difficult
12. movies
13. hospital(s)
14. sleeping
15. although
16. countless
17. scientist(s)
18. species
19. therefore

20. proposal
21. maybe
22. perhaps
23. project
24. collect
25. then
26. them
27. bus
28. during
29. month(s)
30. time
31. later
32. meanwhile
33. hear
34. listen
35. recently
36. believe
37. tale(s)
38. parent(s)
39. misunderstand
40. comment(s)
41. just
42. through
43. describe
44. golden
45. hair
46. rock(s)
47. comb
48. magic
49. underwater
50. creature

20. lifestyle
21. embarrassed
22. information
23. amazing
24. guys
25. destroy
26. crops
27. grasshopper

Expressions: fall in love, Venn Diagram, do not worry, at length final exams, semester break, works better, come across, have nothing against, according to, looking forward, until then, next time

20. play a part
21. to aid
22. honey-bee
23. helpful
24. harmful

Lesson #4—Dragons (Degrees of Adjectives)

1. interested
2. myth(s)
3. interest(s)
4. power point
5. presentation
6. dragon

1. different
2. legend(s)
3. topic(s)
4. help
5. improve
6. language(s)

1. university(ies)
2. research
3. endagared
4. polar bear(s)
5. training
6. freedom

7. winter
8. holiday(s)
9. country(ies)
10. celebrate
11. February
12. folklore

13. mythological
14. which
15. consider
16. smart
17. magic
18. villain(s)
19. exactly
20. obviously
21. fact(s)
22. message(s)
23. call
24. seashell(s)
25. change
26. times
27. ancient
28. purpose(s)
29. harm
30. especially
31. young
32. creature(s)
33. culture(s)
34. to gather
35. partner(s)
36. believe
37. huge
38. real
39. terrible
40. wonderful
41. kill
42. poor
43. large
44. lizard(s)

7. proficiency
8. decide
9. continue
10. discussion(s)
11. prepare
12. understand

13. character(s)
14. famous
15. resilient
16. amazing
17. communicate
18. analyze
19. research
20. researcher(s)
21. puzzled
22. point
23. way(s)
24. today
25. become
26. concern(s)
27. reluctantly
28. agree
29. to intrigue
30. interested
31 describe

Expressions: are (to be) over, getting ready, full of, through ages, each other, long before, digital age, social media

7. role model(s)
8. Santa Claus
9. chimney(ies)
10. capital(s)
11. take part
12. Remembrance Day
13. weekend(s)
14. soldier(s)
15. adjective(s)
16. quality(ies)
17. left
18. historian(s)
19. dictator(s)
20. shark(s)
21. greedy
22. killer
23. prefer
24. grow
25. scale(s)
26. rough

45. beast(s)
46. dangerous
47. cave(s)
48. guard
49. treasure
50. brave
51. terrible
52. hero(es)
53. maturity

Lesson #5-Active Living or Coach Potato (Declarative, Negative and Interrogative Sentences)

1. favorite	1. parent(s)	1. step(s)
2. share	2. brush(es)	2. obese
3. sport	3. different	3. prevent
4. swim	4. healthy	4. associated
5. swimming pool	5. lifestyle(s)	5. popular
6. every day	6. interesting	6. join
7. tennis	7. consider	7. claim
8. usually	8. wonderful	8. world
9. shop	9. analyze	9. nation(s)
10. shopping mall	10. sometimes	10. federation(s)
11. scarf(ves)	11. however	11. competition(s)
12. restaurant(s)	12. reluvtantly	12. enter
13. near	13. continue	13. almost
14. married	14. especially	14. compete
15. hobby(ies)	15. obviously	15. host
16. soccer	16. intrigued	16. competitive
17. watch	17. research	17. qualify
18. match	18. treasure	18. championship(s)
19. wife(ves)	19. protect	19. defensive
20. game(s)	20. guard	20. offensive
21. risk	21. dangerous	21. victorious
22. active	22. resilient	
23. keep	23. way(s)	
24. to exercise	24. topic	
25. regularly		
26. already		
27. fight		

28. obesity
29. also
30. nutritious
31. husband
32. person
33. passive
34. become
35. serious
36. interrupt
37. concept
38. define
39. abnormal
40. excessive
41. accumulation

Expressions: couch potato, instead of, have lunch, take a break

Lesson #6—At the Restaurant (Verb Tenses 1)

1. dish(es)
2. dessert(s)
3. expression(s)
4. dinner(s)
5. night(s)
6. last
7. experience(s)
8. nervous
9. feel
10. comfortable
11. meal(s)
12. invite
13. candle(s)
14. candlestick(s)
15. burn
16. silver
17. elegant
18. gentleman
19. decorate
20. drapes
21. order
22. chicken
23. tomato

1. restaurant(s)
2. different
3. people
4. enjoy
5. nice
6. fruit
7. difficult
8. potato
9. important
10. why
11. when
12. family
13. village
14. however
15. little
16. farm
17. describe
18. house
19. consider
20. way(s)
21. food
22. caterpillar
23. hatch

1. test(s)
2. result(s)
3. toast
4. toaster(s)
5. finally
6. expect
7. answer(s)
8. plant
9. event(s)
10. sequence(s)
11. paragraph(s)
12. indicate
13. complex
14. relationship(s)
15. categorize
16. commonly
17. public
18. transportation
19. wing
20. gem
21. believe

24. salad
25. soup
26. delicious
27. uncomfortable
28. host(s)
29. guest(s)
30. situation(s)
31. honour
32. understand
33. feeling(s)
34. fish
35. hungry
36. anymore
37. slice(s)
38. cheesecake
39. top
40. hospitality
41. tradition(s)
42. culture(s)
43. for example
44. provide
45. the same
46. some
47. poor
48. belong
49. normal
50. special
51. offer
52. scarce
53. appreciate
54. sharing

Expressions: to have a sweet tooth, have dinner, save some space, am not sure, grow up

Lesson #7—When the Sun Went Away (Verb Tenses 2)

1. goddess	1. elegant	1. action
2. god	2. gentleman	2. repeated
3. satisfied	3. feeling	3. doll
4. progress	4. nervous	4. attention
5. crop	5. proficiency	5. completely
6. reflect	6. appreciate	6. look up

7. evil
8. spirit
9. to fear
10. jealous
11. subject
12. to plan
13. step
14. call
15. temple
16. self-confidence
17. slow
18. huge
19. snake
20. usually
21. classmate
22. destroy
23. frighten
24. self-confident
25. intimidated
26. fluent
27. curious
28. beat
29. drum
30. ring (rang)
31. bell
32. supportive
33. to master
34. teammates
35. explain
36. proud
37. follow
38. earth
39. dramatically
40. hide
41. representative
42. wise
43. promise
44. remarkable

7. share
8. answer
9. culture
10. uncomfortable
11. honour
12. exactly
13. legend
14. believe
15. harm
16. dark
17. cave
18. surrounded
19. bright
20. special
21. way
22. enjoy(able)

7. almost
8. kitten
9. bowl
10. pick up
11. delighted
12. reply
13. purred
14. concentration
15. span
16. wandering
17. brain
18. increase
19. giraffe
20. tongue

Expressions: do(ing) fine, nothing to worry about, speak highly of (somebody), clear the throat, grow jealous, go away, to be scared, beat a drum, ring a bell, feel sorry

Lesson #8—Thanksgiving (This & That)

1. Thanksgiving
2. celebration
3. roast
4. turkey
5. climate
6. bakery(ies)
7. owner
8. order
9. characteristic
10. settler
11. wedding
12. survive
13. fancy
14. survival
15. amazed
16. skill
17. nothing
18. compare
19. easy
20. either
21. mountain
22. valley
23. muddy
24. arrive
25. behind
26. check
27. mean(v)
28. stress(v)
29. harvest
30. simple
31. October
32. November
33. Explorer
34. passage
35. formal
36. ceremony
37. journey
38. cross(v)

1. plan(v)
2. dinner
3. culture
4. reflect
5. self-confidence
6. remarkable
7. crops
8. earth
9. food
10. master(v)
11. explain
12. call
13 lifestyle
14. experience
15. however
16. enjoyable
17. pull a cart
18. interesting
19. anybody
20. anything
21. share
22. information
23. satisfied
24. celebrate
25. invite
26. consider
27. cheesecake
28. neighbourhood
29. ancient
30. usually

1. tax
2. coat
3. price
4. busy
5. blood
6. pressure
7. cheat
8. fix
9. necessary
10. weekend
11. boots
12. expensive
13. acceptable

Expressions: (to be) is around the corner, on the eve of, due to, to be confused, ride a horse

307

39. feast
40. ocean
41. huge
42. include
43. encounter
44. interchangeably
45. chef
46. distinguish
47. imply
48. heat
49. prefer
50. dry
51. specifically
52. poultry
53. starch
54. surface
55. attractive
56. crispy
57. crust
58. cranberry
59. evidence
60. pumpkin
61. grain
62. paste
63. household
64. oven
65. steam
66. stuffing

THEME #2—SPECIAL PEOPLE, SPECIAL DEEDS

<u>Lesson #1—Town Hero</u> (Articles)

1. tracks	1. classmate	1. firefighter
2. derailment	2. difficult	2. rescue
3. commuters	3. improve	3. assisst
4. announce	4. dramatically	4. freezing
5. major	5. weekend	5. ice-choked

6. weather
7. headache
8. safe
9. delay
10. throughout
11. faint
12. extreme
13. swerve
14. fast
15. rush
16. region
17. contribute
18. accident
19. driveway
20. deed
21. centimeter
22. combine (with . . .)
23. block
24. railway
25. service
26. crash
27. hero
28. driver
29. wheel
30. rush
31. street
32. icy
33. frozen
34. instantly
35. turn
36. examine
37. conclude
38. act

6. ride
7. usual
8. understand
9. due to
10. climate
11. health
12. condition
13. danger
14. decision
15. push
16. sick
17. cause
18. dangerous
19. distinguish
20. team
21. include
22. respond

6. helicopter
7. perform
8. daring
9. particular
10. mention
11. merited
12. leap
13. incredible
14. circumstances
15. literally
16. risk
17deserve
18. praise
19. commendation
20. particular
21. emergency

Expressions: weather forecast, brought to a safe stop, run away bus, get hurt, steering wheel, brake pedal, slow down

Lesson #2—Vote of Confidence (Direct & Indirect Speech)

1. representation
2. significant
3. issue
4. politics

1. major
2. service
3. announce
4. extreme

1. message
2. set off
3. previous
4. resign

5. elect
6. election
7. although
8. female
9. increase
10. party
11. to date
12. achieve
13. gender
14. parity
15. nominate
16. main
17. retired
18. journalist
19. determine
20. perspective
21. partner
22. democracy
23. pressure
24. appoint
25. tremendous
26. gains
27. financial
28. security
29. maintain
30. secure
31. to rank
32. national
33. federal
34. provincial
35. parliament
36. government
37. population
38. municipal
39. under-representation
40. academics
41. media
42. despite
43. poll

5. contribute
6. examine
7. conclude
8. act
9. province
10. distinguished
11. improve
12. situation
13. stress
14. important
15. however
16. representative
17. circle
18. invite
19. medicine
20. enter
21. situation
22. belief
23. dismal
24. career
25. promote
26. intervention

5. agreement
6. skiing
7. administrator
8. regard
9. model
10. propose
11. astonished
12. account
13. exchange
14. cabinet
15. vehemently
16. failure
17. public
18. prime minister
19. permit
20. bravely
21. shuffle
22. portfolio

Expressions: House of Commons, fare share, in terms of, reach a plateau, according to, glass ceiling, change the face of . . . .

44. conduct
45. to state
46. plateau
47. hover
48. facilitate
49. level

Lesson #3—A Marathon of Hope (Passive Voice & Story Timeline)

1. raise
2. athletic
3. tender
4. age
5. diagnose
6. bone
7. cancer
8. to force
9. amputate
10. hospitalize
11. to witness
12. suffering
13. patient
14. funding
15. limited
16. motivate
17. cure
18. seriously
19. journey
20. marathon
21. eventually
22. collect
23. route
24. to mount to . . . .
25. unfortunately
26. kilometers
27. appear
28. lung
29. entire
30. nation
31. stunned

1. young
2. invlove
3. dangerous
4. disease
5. weast coast
6. centimeter
7. especially
8. research
9. although
10. sick
11. accross
12. decide
13. money
14. get ready
15. nobody
16. enthusiasm
17. however
18. province
19. examine
20. decide
21. health
22. problem
23. to date
24. special
25. organization
26. maintain
27. government
28. join
29. representation
30. consist of . . . .
31. important

1. instruct
2. identify
3. timetable
4. schedule
5. chronology
6. particular
7. historical
8. illustrative
9. visual
10. accompanied
11. commentary
12. arrange
13. keep track

32. saddened
33. legacy
34. worldwide
35. annual
36. create
37. strive
38. effort
39. integrity
40. embody
41. seek
42. administration
43. fundraising
44. cost
45. grant
46. temporary
47. distribute
48. inspire
49. decade

32. celebrate

Expressions: estrogenic sarcoma, raise funds, pay attention to, shocking news, pass away, live on.

Lesson #4-Doctor Without Borders (Personal Response)

1. attend	1. country	1. relevant
2. interrupt	2. anybody	2. specialist
3. lumber	3. medical	3. commitment
4. enlist	4. patient	4. responsibility
5. tuberculosis (TBC)	5. service	5. look for
6. demand	6. determined	6. unique
7. divorce	7. accept	7. express
8. inevitable	8. lung	8. regarding
9. waste	9. temorarely	9. opinion
10. frequently	10. cure	10. relate to . . . .
11. controversial	11. patient	11. possible
12. treatment	12. conditions	12. tap into
13. artificial	13. medicine	13. pretend
14. collapse	14. equal	14. conflict
15. permanently	15. government	15. dialogue
16. recover	16. however	16. pertinent
17. surgery	17. receive	17. airmen
18. surgeon	18. (un)popular	18. contribution
19. crowded	19. difficult	19. mankind

20. unsanitary
21. proper
22. socialized
23. progressive
24. reaction
25. radical
26. ranging
27. spokesman
28. to head
29. top paid
30. pioneering
31. transfusion
32. wound
33. mobile
34. contain
35. dressing
36. supplies
37. mule
38. occasion
39. invader
40. prodigious
41. rate
42. artillery
43. extraordinary
44. undaunted
45. rubber
46. bacteria
47. penetrate
48. refuse
49. poisoning
50. humanitarian
51. recognition
52. impact
53. erect
54. extol
55. restore
56. dedicate
57. unselfish
58. remain

20. decision
21. blood
22. become
23. unfortunately
24. dangerous
25. medication
26. throughout
27. destroyed
28. include
29. information
30. creative
31. particular
32. journalist
33. deed

20. invent
21. refine
22. infection
23. tribute
24. essay

Expressions: set up, stretcher bearer, give up on himself, bomb shelter, compression therapy, was aware of

Lesson #5—Braille Alphabet (Paragraph Writing & Topic Sentence)

1. introduce	1. discussion	1. coherent
2. encounter	2. enter	2. related
3. interesting	3. sick	3. grasp
4. invent	4. feeling	4. general
5. blind	5. enjoyable	5. illustration
6. flu	6. reaction	6. describe
7. cough	7. reluctantly	7. brief
8. miss	8. popular	8. narrate
9. manage	9. become	9. contrast
10. contribute	10. especially	10. classify
11. normal	11. throat	11. cause
12. complain	12. special	12. regardless
13. complement	13. creative	13. support
14. comment	14. interested	14. . unify
15. guess	15. letters	15. determine
16. absence	16. everyone	16. perspective
17. sore	17. information	17. effective
18. avoid	18. different	18. current
19. suggestion	19. everybody	19. previous
20. communicate	20. distribute	20. majority
21. outfit	21. pronunciation	21. common
22. blush	22. sentence	22. genetic
23. genuinely	23. definition	23. disorder
24. embossed	24. due to	24. gene
25. typed	25. hurt	25. abnormal
26. adapt	26. wound	26. mucus
27. notation	27. infect	27. clog
28. elevator	28. infection	28. respiratory
29. gather	29. share	29. complication
30. paragraph	30. raise	30. blockage
31. check	31. although	31. bronchial
32. dictionary	32. difficult	32. passage
33. explain	33. battlefield	33. permanent
34. proudly	34. amazed	34. trap
35. forever	35. extraordinary	35. duct
36. harness	36. inspire	36. enzyme
37. workshop	37. contain	37. digestion
38. grab	38. example	38. tent

39. sharp
40. tool
41. hole
42. to slide
43. spread
44. lose
45. scholarship
46. library
47. huge
48. impatient
49. former
50. code
51. dot
52. bump
53. trim
54. publish
55. skeptical
56. graduate
57. worldwide
58. practically
59. prove
60. pattern
61. skip
62. independently
63. incredible
64. constellation

39. event
40. compare
41. effect
42. characteristics
43. important
44. thick
45. lung
46. responsible
47. destroy
48. bacteria
49. master
50. jealous

39. blanket
40. gossip
41. warranty

Expressions: partially sighted, index card, figure out, top-secret, went(go) very wrong all of a sudden, things were looking up, iron put, on their own, took(take) up the cause, get around

Task #2—Read the story about Thomas Edison and find points that you can compare to the stories you read in this textbook.

Thomas Alva Edison lit up the world with his invention of the electric light. Without him, the world might still be a dark place. However, the electric light was not his only invention. He also invented the phonograph, the motion picture camera, and over 1,200 other things. About every two weeks he created something new.

Thomas A. Edison was born in Milan, Ohio, on February 11, 1847. His family moved to Port Huron, Michigan, when he was seven years old. Surprisingly, he attended school for only two months. His mother, a former teacher, taught him a few things, but Thomas was mostly self-educated. His natural curiosity led him to start experimenting at a young age with electrical and mechanical things at home.

When he was 12 years old, he got his first job. He became a newsboy on a train that ran between Port Huron and Detroit. He set up a laboratory in a baggage car of the train so that he could continue his experiments in his spare time. Unfortunately, his first work experience did not end well. Thomas was fired when he accidentally set fire to the floor of the baggage car.

Thomas then worked for five years as a telegraph operator, but he continued to spend much of his time on the job conducting experiments. He got his first patent in 1868 for a vote recorder run by electricity. However, the vote recorder was not a success. In 1870, he sold another invention, a stock-ticker, for $40,000. A stock-ticker is a machine that automatically prints stock prices on a tape. He was then able to build his first shop in Newark, New Jersey.

Thomas Edison was totally deaf in one ear and hard of hearing in the other, but thought of his deafness as a blessing in many ways. It kept conversations short, so that he could have more time for work. He called himself a "two-shift man" because he worked 16 out of every 24 hours. Sometimes he worked so intensely that his wife had to remind him to sleep and eat. Thomas Edison died at the age of 84 on October 18, 1931, at his estate in West Orange, New Jersey. He left numerous inventions that improved the quality of life all over the world.

- . . . .
. . . .
. . . .
. . . .
- . . . .
. . . .
. . . .
. . . .

. . . .
. . . .
. . . .
. . . .
. . . .
. . . .
. . . .
. . . .

Task #3—Choose the correct answer and circle the letter with the correct answer (a, b, c, or d)

1. Thomas Edison did things in this order in his life:
   a. he became a telegraph operator, a newsboy, and then got his first patent
   b. he became a newsboy, got his first patent, and then became a telegraph operator
   c. he got a patent, became a telegraph operator, and then became a newsboy
   d. he became a newsboy, a telegraph operator, and then got a patent

2. Edison considered his deafness:
   a. a disadvantage
   b. a blessing
   c. something from a priest
   d. a necessity

3. Of all the inventions, _____ was probably the most important for civilization.
   a. the vote recorder
   b. the stock ticker
   c. the light bulb
   d. the motion picture camera

4. The main idea of this passage is:
   a. Thomas Edison could not keep a job.

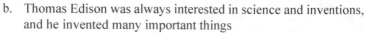

b. Thomas Edison was always interested in science and inventions, and he invented many important things

c. Thomas Edison worked day and night on his experiments.

d. Deaf people make good inventors because they can focus without the distraction of spoken conversation.

5. Edison thought he benefitted from his deafness because:
   a. he had more time to read
   b. he became more fluent
   c. he wouldn't waste his time talking
   d. he would be knowledgeable in different fields

Task #4—Answer the following questions:

1. For how long did Thomas Edison attend school? . . . .
. . . .
. . . .
. . . .
. . . .
. . . .

2. In what states and cities of the USA did he live and work? . . . .
. . . .
. . . .
. . . .
. . . .

3. Who was Thomas Edison's main teacher? . . . .
. . . .
. . . .
. . . .
. . . .

4. Where was Edison's first laboratory? . . . .
. . . .
. . . .
. . . .

5. How did Edison handle his physical handicap? . . . .
. . . .
. . . .
. . . .
. . . .

Task #5—Choose the correct answer (and circle the letter a, b, c, or d) that means the same as the underlined word or phrase in the sentence.

1. His mother, a former teacher, taught him a few things, but he was mostly <u>self-educated</u>.
   a. taught himself
   b. born a genius
   c. loved school
   d. thought of himself

2. His natural curiosity soon led him to start <u>experimenting</u> with electrical and mechanical things at home.
   a. experiencing
   b. inventing
   c. making tests and playing with
   d. ignoring

3. He left <u>numerous</u> inventions that improved the quality of life all over the world.
   a. numbered
   b. many
   c. none
   d. modern

4. Sometimes he worked so <u>intensely</u> that his wife had to remind him to sleep and eat.
   a. passionately and with great focus
   b. carelessly and with many distractions
   c. hard
   d. problems

5. He set his first <u>laboratory</u> in a baggage car.
   a. a room without windows
   b. a place to relax
   c. a place for research
   d. the room in the basement

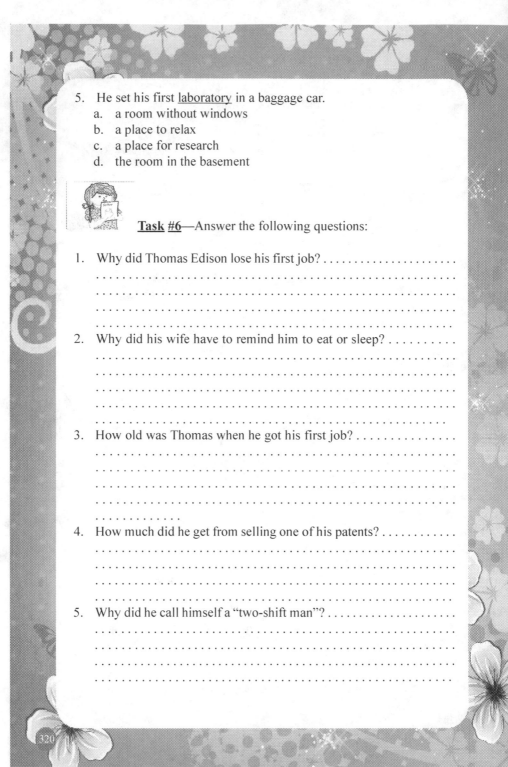

Task #6—Answer the following questions:

1. Why did Thomas Edison lose his first job? . . . .
. . . .
. . . .
. . . .

2. Why did his wife have to remind him to eat or sleep? . . . .
. . . .
. . . .
. . . .
. . . .

3. How old was Thomas when he got his first job? . . . .
. . . .
. . . .
. . . .
. . . .
. . . .

4. How much did he get from selling one of his patents? . . . .
. . . .
. . . .
. . . .
. . . .

5. Why did he call himself a "two-shift man"? . . . .
. . . .
. . . .
. . . .
. . . .

Task #7—Write a letter to a friend explaining to him how extraordinary and inspiring Thomas Edison's life is to you. Compare his life to other heroes you know or have read about in Fun English 5. You need to write at least three paragraphs, use correct grammar, clear thoughts, good punctuation and spelling. Pay attention to paragraph structure and write a Topic Sentence for each paragraph.

Progress Exam

Task #1—Find the correct definition for the words below and write a sentence with each word: **20 POINTS**

ancient_____

_____

myth_____

_____

swerve_____

_____

amputate_____

_____

obesity_____

_____

witness_____

_____

research_____

_____

nutrituous_____

_____

stunned_____

_____

legacy_____

_____

annual_____

_____

delicious_____

_____

remarkable_____

_____

representative_____

settler_____

harvest_____

derailment_____

major_____

significant_____

tremendous_____

Task #2—Circle "T" if a sentence is true. Circle "N" if a sentence is not true. Circle "X" if you do not understand the sentence. **10 POINTS**

T (This is **True**) N (This is **Not true**) X (I do **Not understand** the question)

1. This triangle is little.   **T N X**

2. You can find these buildings
    everywhere   **T N X**
3. Many people have their arm amputated.   **T N X**
4. The word "swerve" in the sentence: The bus began
    to "swerve"—means "show me how to do it".   **T N X**
5. "Train derailment" means "an express train".   **T N X**

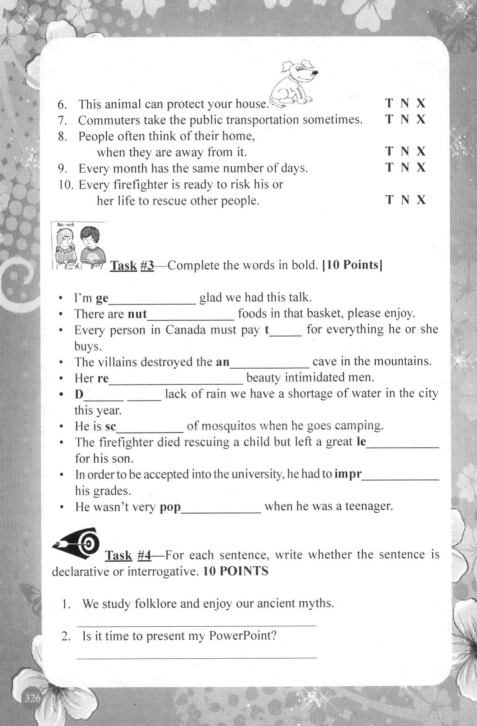

6. This animal can protect your house.　　　　　**T N X**
7. Commuters take the public transportation sometimes.　**T N X**
8. People often think of their home,
　　when they are away from it.　　　　　　**T N X**
9. Every month has the same number of days.　　**T N X**
10. Every firefighter is ready to risk his or
　　her life to rescue other people.　　　　　**T N X**

Task #3—Complete the words in bold. **[10 Points]**

- I'm **ge**_____ glad we had this talk.
- There are **nut**_____ foods in that basket, please enjoy.
- Every person in Canada must pay **t**_____ for everything he or she buys.
- The villains destroyed the **an**_____ cave in the mountains.
- Her **re**_____ beauty intimidated men.
- **D**_____ _____ lack of rain we have a shortage of water in the city this year.
- He is **sc**_____ of mosquitos when he goes camping.
- The firefighter died rescuing a child but left a great **le**_____ for his son.
- In order to be accepted into the university, he had to **impr**_____ his grades.
- He wasn't very **pop**_____ when he was a teenager.

Task #4—For each sentence, write whether the sentence is declarative or interrogative. **10 POINTS**

1. We study folklore and enjoy our ancient myths.

_____

2. Is it time to present my PowerPoint?

_____

3. Why should we punish an entire nation for the doing of a few people?

_____

4. We meet at a restaurant for a nutritious meal every Saturday.

_____

5. We enjoy studying the amazing deeds of our heroes.

_____

6. Where is the money going to come from?

_____

7. Traffic clogs the roads.

_____

8. The crowds had begun to gather into the place by 8 p.m. to talk to their representative.

_____

9. Who knows when it was made?

_____

10. How many caves like that are left in the world?

_____

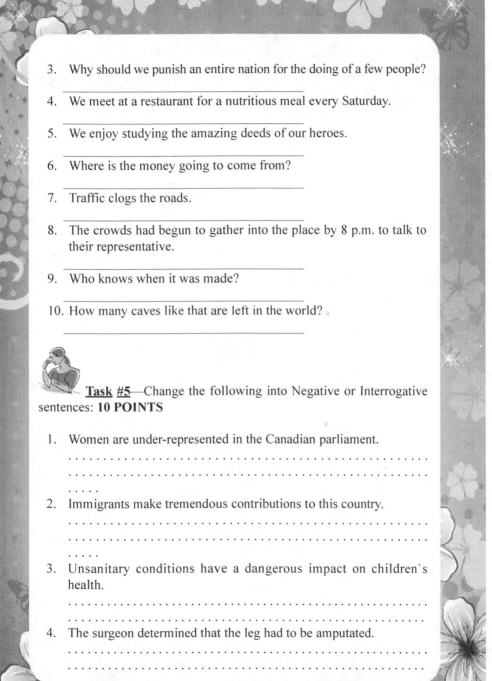

Task #5—Change the following into Negative or Interrogative sentences: **10 POINTS**

1. Women are under-represented in the Canadian parliament.

. . . .
. . . .
. . . . .

2. Immigrants make tremendous contributions to this country.

. . . .
. . . .
. . . . .

3. Unsanitary conditions have a dangerous impact on children's health.

. . . .
. . . .

4. The surgeon determined that the leg had to be amputated.

. . . .
. . . .

5. Noel and Nick wrote a remarkable personal response to the story.

   . . . .
   . . . .

6. George and Monique found the test very difficult.

   . . . .
   . . . .

7. Stephen and Paolo are very good neighbors.

   . . . .
   . . . .

8. She was very active in the fundraising as she was inspired by her hero.

   . . . .
   . . . .
   . . . . .

9. They nominated their partner for the new election.

   . . . .
   . . . .
   . . . . .

10. The extreme weather created difficulties in driving instantly.

   . . . .
   . . . .
   . . . . .

Task #6—Answer the following questions using a Possessive Form of the word in brackets: **10 POINTS**

1. Whose umbrella is it? (the teacher). . . . .
   . . . .

2. Whose bicycle is it? (Mr. Knowitall). . . . .
. . . .

3. Whose guitar is it? (Monique). . . . .
. . . .

4. Whose watering-can is it? (Karen). . . . .
. . . .

5. Whose toys are they? (your children). . . . .
. . . .

6. Whose patient is he? (the doctor). . . . .
. . . .

7. Whose glasses are they? (my grandmother). . . . .
. . . .

8. Whose drapes are they? (an Italian actor). . . . .
. . . .

9.  Whose watches are they? (our friends). . . . .
. . . .

10. Whose house is it? (my grandparents). . . . .
. . . .

Task #7—Read the story about Florence Nightingale and answer the question that follow the story. **20 POINTS**

Florence Nightingale **"The Lady of the Lamp"**

Florence Nightingale was a truly inspirational nurse. Florence Nightingale is famous for her medical work during Crimean War (1854-1856). She changed the medical services from an untrained profession to a highly skilled and well-respected medical profession with very important responsibilities.

Florence Nightingale was born on 12 May 1820 in Florence, Italy. She was named after the city of her birth. Both her parents were strong fighters for the abolition of slavery. Florence Nightingale had a broad education and came to dislike the lack of opportunity for females in her social circle. She began to visit the poor but became very interested in looking after those who were ill. She visited hospitals in London and around the country to investigate possible jobs for women there. However, nursing was seen as employment that needed neither study nor intelligence; nurses were considered to be little less than prostitutes at that time.

Nightingale's hospital visits began in 1844 and continued for eleven years. She spent the winter and spring of 1849 in Egypt with family friends. Her visit convinced Nightingale of the possibilities of making nursing a remarkable job for ladies. When she returned home, she undertook more visits to London hospitals; in the autumn of 1852 she inspected hospitals in Edinburgh and Dublin. In 1853 she accepted her first administrative post when she became superintendent of the Hospital for Invalid Gentlewomen.

In September 1856 Nightingale visited Queen Victoria at Balmoral and told the Queen and Prince Albert about everything that 'affects our present military hospital system and the reforms that are needed'. In November 1855 a Nightingale fund had been set up to found a training school for nurses. This was the only recognition of her services of which Nightingale would approve. By 1860, £50,000 had been collected and the Nightingale School and Home for Nurses was established at St. Thomas's Hospital.

Florence Nightingale traveled to Europe to study the European hospital system. In 1850 she traveled to Alexandria, Egypt, and began studying nursing. She went to Germany to train as a nurse in 1851. She received was the Order of Merit in 1907 and in 1908 she was awarded the Freedom of the City of London award. She had already received the German order of the Cross of Merit and the French gold medal in 1909. On 10 May 1910 she was presented with the badge of honour of the Norwegian Red Cross Society.

Florence Nightingale was very dedicated to her job. She would often visit the soldiers at night when everyone was asleep just to make sure they were OK. She was referred to as "The Lady of the Lamp". She became a true hero to the soldiers and everyone in England. Nightingale died in London, on 13 August 1910 at the age of ninety.

Answer these questions:

- Who was Florence Nightingale? . . . .
. . . .
. . . .
. . . .

- What is the contribution she gave to medicine? . . . .
. . . .
. . . .
. . . .
. . . .

- Do you think it was easy for her to be a nurse? Why? . . . .
. . . .

. . . .
. . . .
. . . .

• What gave her the name "The Lady of the Lamp"? . . . .
. . . .
. . . .
. . . .
. . . .

• Does this story remind you of any of the heroes you read about in this
book? Which one? . . . .
. . . .
. . . .
. . . .

Task #8—Read the Florence Nightingale story again.
Make a timeline of her life starting with her date of her birth and ending
with her date of death. Make sure each year and activity is reflected in the
timeline. **10 POINTS**

CONGRATULATIONS!

END OF BOOK #5

(You can proceed to book #6 if your test score is 85% or more)

HELPFUL DEFINITIONS AND RULES

- ❖ A **compound word** is a word made up of two or more words. e. x. doghouse, sandbox, milkman
- ❖ A **root word** is a word to which a prefix or suffix may be added to form a new word. e. x. **print**(er), **pack**(age), (a)**like**
- ❖ A **suffix** is an addition made at the end of a root word. e. x. print(**s**), pack(**ing**), like(**d**)
- ○ When a word ends in "y" preceded by a consonant, change the **"y"** into **"i"** before adding a suffix other than **"ing"**. e. x. cry**(ing)**, try**(ing)**
- ○ A suffix is a syllable in itself if it contains a vowel. e.x. kind**ness**, fly**ing**, warm**er**,
- ○ When a word ends in a silent "e", drop "e" before adding a suffix that begins with a vowel. E.x. hik(es), skat(es), receiv(es), fin(er), pur(er)
- ○ When a word ends in a single consonant preceded by a short vowel sound, usually double the consonant before adding a suffix that begins with a vowel. E.x. rip(ped), jump(ping), big(ger), fat(ter), ho(ter), tip(ping)
- ❖ A **prefix** is a syllable that is added to the beginning of the root word. e. x. (**re**)print, (**un**)pack, (**dis**)like
- ○ The prefix "re" usually means "do again". E.x. repaint, rebuild, refill, rewrite, reload
- ○ The prefix "de' usually means "from". e.x. depart, detour, derail, deice, depart
- ○ The prefix "ex" usually means "out of" or "from". E.x. export, exchange,
- ○ The prefixes "un" and "dis" usually means "not". e.x. dishonest, displease, uncertain, unfair, distrust, disagree, unseen, unload, dislocate, unfold, unpin, discharge, disunite, disclose, disappear, unhappy, unsafe, unchain

PLURAL OF NOUNS

❖ To make a word mean more than one:
○ Usually add **"s"**—cat**(s)**, dogs**(s)**, kite**(s)**, book**(s)**, girl**(s)**, teacher**(s)**, flower**(s)**, clown**(s)**, boy**(s)**, classroom**(s)**
○ Usually add **"es"** if a noun ends in x, z, ss, sh, or ch—fox**(es)**, buss(es), peach(es), dress(es), bush(es), brush(es), church(es), six(es), ax(es)
○ Usually change **"y"** into **"i"** and add **"es"** to nouns that end in **"y"** preceded by a consonant. e. x. country **(ies)**, party **(ies)**, sky **(ies)**, baby **(ies)**.
○ But add only **"s"** to nouns that end in **"y"** preceded by a vowel. e. x. day**(s)**, boy**(s)**, toy**(s)**, guy**(s)**
○ Usually add **"es"** to nouns that end with **"o"**. e. x. hero**(es)**, patato**(es)**, tomato**(es)**. But add only **"s"** to some nous. e. x. piano**(s)**
○ Usually nouns that the nouns that end in **"ef"** or **"fe"** form the plural by adding **"ves"**. E.x. leaf—leaves, knife-knives, wife-wives, life-lives, elf-elves, half-halves
○ Some nouns that have "oo" between to consonants change that into "ee" in plural form. E.x. tooth-teeth, goose—geese.
○ Some nouns do not follow rules to form the plural. e. x. man-men, child-children, woman-women, ox-oxen, mouse-mice
○ Some nouns are always used in plural. e. x. trousers, glasses, spectacles,
○ There are some nouns that are never used in plural. e. x. sheep, deer, fish

IRREGULAR VERBS CHART

Infinitive	Simple Present	Simple Past	Past Participle	Present Participle
to arise	arise(s)	Arose	arisen	Arising
to awake	awake(s)	awoke *or* awaked	awaked *or* awoken	Awaking
to be	am, is, are	was, were	been	Being
to bear	bear(s)	bore	borne *or* born	Bearing
to beat	beat(s)	beat	beaten	Beating
to become	become(s)	became	become	becoming
to begin	begin(s)	began	begun	beginning
to bend	bend(s)	bent	bent	bending
to bet	bet(s)	bet	bet	betting
to bid [*to offer*]	bid(s)	bid	bid	bidding
to bid [*to command*]	bid(s)	bade	bidden	bidding
to bind	bind(s)	bound	bound	binding
to bite	bite(s)	bit	bitten *or* bit	biting

to blow	blow(s)	blew	blown	blowing
to break	break(s)	broke	broken	breaking
to bring	bring(s)	brought	brought	bringing
to build	build(s)	built	built	building
to burst	burst(s)	burst	burst	bursting
to buy	buy(s)	bought	bought	buying
to cast	cast(s)	cast	cast	casting
to catch	catch(es)	caught	caught	catching
to choose	choose(s)	chose	chosen	choosing
to cling	cling(s)	clung	clung	clinging
to come	come(s)	came	come	coming
to cost	cost(s)	cost	cost	costing
to creep	creep(s)	crept	crept	creeping
to cut	cut(s)	cut	cut	cutting
to deal	deal(s)	dealt	dealt	dealing
to dig	dig(s)	dug	dug	digging
to dive	dive(s)	dived *or* dove	dived	diving
to do	do(es)	did	done	doing
to draw	draw(s)	drew	drawn	drawing
to dream	dream(s)	dreamed *or* dreamt	dreamed *or* dreamt	dreaming
to drink	drink(s)	drank	drunk	drinking
to drive	drive(s)	drove	driven	driving
to eat	eat(s)	ate	eaten	eating
to fall	fall(s)	fell	fallen	falling
to feed	feed(s)	fed	fed	Feeding
to feel	feel(s)	felt	felt	Feeling
to fight	fight(s)	fought	fought	Fighting
to find	find(s)	found	found	Finding
to flee	flee(s)	fled	fled	Fleeing
to fling	fling(s)	flung	flung	Flinging
to fly	flies, fly	flew	flown	Flying
to forbid	forbid(s)	forbade *or* forbad	forbidden	Forbidding

337

to forget	forget(s)	forgot	forgotten *or* forgot	Forgetting
to forgive	forgive(s)	forgave	forgiven	Forgiving
to forsake	forsake(s)	forsook	forsaken	Forsaking
to freeze	freeze(s)	froze	frozen	Freezing
to get	get(s)	got	got *or* gotten	Getting
to give	give(s)	gave	given	Giving
to go	go(es)	went	gone	Going
to grow	grow(s)	grew	grown	Growing
to hang [*to suspend*]	hang(s)	hung	hung	Hanging
to have	has, have	had	had	Having
to hear	hear(s)	heard	heard	Hearing
to hide	hide(s)	hid	hidden	Hiding
to hit	hit(s)	hit	hit	Hitting
to hurt	hurt(s)	Hurt	hurt	Hurting
to keep	keep(s)	kept	kept	Keeping
to know	know(s)	knew	known	Knowing
to lay	lay(s)	laid	laid	Laying
to lead	lead(s)	led	led	Leading
to leap	leap(s)	leaped *or* leapt	leaped *or* leapt	Leaping
to leave	leave(s)	left	left	Leaving
to lend	lend(s)	lent	lent	Lending
to let	let(s)	let	let	Letting
to lie [*to rest*]	lie(s)	lay	lain	Lying
to light	light(s)	lighted *or* lit	lighted *or* lit	Lighting
to lose	lose(s)	lost	lost	Losing
to make	make(s)	made	made	Making
to mean	mean(s)	meant	meant	Meaning
to pay	pay(s)	paid	paid	Paying
to prove	prove(s)	proved	proved *or* proven	Proving
to quit	quit(s)	quit	quit	Quitting
to read	read(s)	read	read	Reading

to rid	rid(s)	rid	rid	Ridding
to ride	ride(s)	rode	ridden	Riding
to ring	ring(s)	rang	rung	Ringing
to rise	rise(s)	rose	risen	Rising
to run	run(s)	ran	run	Running
to say	say(s)	said	said	Saying
to see	see(s)	saw	seen	Seeing
to seek	seek(s)	sought	sought	Seeking
to send	send(s)	sent	sent	Sending
to set	set(s)	set	set	Setting
to shake	shake(s)	shook	shaken	Shaking
to shine [*to glow*]	shine(s)	shone	shone	Shining
to shoot	shoot(s)	shot	shot	Shooting
to show	show(s)	showed	shown *or* showed	Showing
to shrink	shrink(s)	shrank	shrunk	Shrinking
to sing	sing(s)	sang	sung	Singing
to sink	sink(s)	sank *or* sunk	sunk	Sinking
to sit	sit(s)	sat	sat	Sitting
to slay	slay(s)	slew	slain	Slaying
to sleep	sleep(s)	slept	slept	Sleeping
to sling	sling(s)	slung	slung	Slinging
to sneak	sneak(s)	sneaked *or* snuck	sneaked *or* snuck	Sneaking
to speak	speak(s)	spoke	spoken	Speaking
to spend	spend(s)	spent	spent	Spending
to spin	spin(s)	spun	spun	Spinning
to spring	spring(s)	sprang *or* sprung	sprung	Springing
to stand	stand(s)	stood	stood	Standing
to steal	steal(s)	stole	stolen	Stealing
to sting	sting(s)	stung	stung	Stinging
to stink	stink(s)	stank *or* stunk	stunk	Stinking
to stride	stride(s)	strode	stridden	Striding

to strike	strike(s)	struck	struck	Striking
to strive	strive(s)	strove	striven	Striving
to swear	swear(s)	swore	sworn	Swearing
\to sweep	sweep(s)	swept	swept	Sweeping
to swim	swim(s)	swam	swum	Swimming
to swing	swing(s)	swung	swung	Swinging
to take	take(s)	took	taken	Taking
to teach	teach(es)	taught	taught	Teaching
to tear	tear(s)	tore	torn	Tearing
to tell	tell(s)	told	told	Telling
to think	think(s)	thought	thought	Thinking
to throw	throw(s)	threw	thrown	Throwing
to understand	understand(s)	understood	understood	understanding
to wake	wake(s)	woke *or* waked	waked *or* woken	Waking
to wear	wear(s)	wore	worn	Wearing
to weave	weave(s)	wove *or* weaved	woven *or* wove	Weaving
to weep	weep(s)	wept	wept	Weeping
to wring	wring(s)	wrung	wrung	Wringing
to write	write(s)	wrote	written	Writing

Recommended novel for a book report:

TITLE:	Helen Keller—Crusader for the Blind and Deaf
AUTHORS:	Stewart & Polly Ann Graff
PUBLICATION:	Bantam Doubleday Dell Books for Young Readers, (1991) 1540 Broadway New York, New York 10036 ISBN: 0-440-40439-8